WALKS FOR ALL AGES
CORNWALL

WALKS FOR
ALL AGES

CORNWALL

JOHN & VICKY WOOD

BRADWELL
BOOKS

Published by Bradwell Books
9 Orgreave Close Sheffield S13 9NP
Email: books@bradwellbooks.co.uk
© John & Vicky Wood 2014

British Library Cataloguing in Publication Data: a catalogue record for this
book is available from the British Library.

1st Edition

ISBN: 9781902674780

Print: Gomer Press, Llandysul, Ceredigion SA44 4JL

Design by: Erik Siewko Creative, Derbyshire.
eriksiewko@gmail.com

Photograph Credits: © Vicky Wood 2014

Maps: Contain Ordnance Survey data
© Crown copyright and database right 2014

Ordnance Survey licence number 100039353

The information in this book has been produced in good faith and is intended
as a general guide. Bradwell Books and its authors have made all reasonable
efforts to ensure that the details are correct at the time of publication.
Bradwell Books and the author cannot accept any responsibility for any
changes that have taken place subsequent to the book being published.
It is the responsibility of individuals undertaking any of the walks listed in
this publication to exercise due care and consideration for the health and
wellbeing of each other in the party. Particular care should be taken if you
are inexperienced. The walks in this book are not especially strenuous but
individuals taking part should ensure they are fit and able to complete the
walk before setting off.

WALKS FOR ALL AGES

INTRODUCTION

Anyone who has visited the magical county of Cornwall will have noticed that it has no mountains. The more observant will have noticed also that there are no flat bits!

It was a challenge, therefore, to be asked to choose 20 short walks suitable for all ages with a minimum of stiles and steep gradients.

Fortunately, having walked all of coastal (and most of inland) Cornwall with two friends and their energetic spaniel, we had a great many beautiful walks to choose from. Those that follow, whilst being far from flat or stile free, are reasonably easy and amongst our favourites.

They vary in length between two and four miles and where possible we have identified alternative shorter walks for those wishing to take an easier route.
It goes without saying that walkers must take responsibility for their own health and safety. Many walks are alongside high cliffs, which can be dangerous for children and for dogs, and you are advised to be extra cautious during the wet when paths can become muddy and slippery.

LISTEN FOR THE GHOSTS OF MINERS AND SMUGGLERS, AND LEARN OF MERMAIDS AND GIANTS AS YOU EXPLORE CORNWALL'S LONELY CRAGS AND CREEKS, ITS RUINED ENGINE HOUSES AND MOSSY TRAMWAYS.

Adders like to sunbathe in amongst Cornish rocks and can pose a danger to inquisitive dogs or toddlers. We advise you always to wear sensible clothing and shoes and to take an Ordnance Survey map, compass and mobile phone. Weather conditions, especially on the moors, can change quickly so get a good forecast and be prepared for the worst.

For those with a sat-nav we have included postcodes to help you find the start of the walk but please note that they may not relate exactly to the car park. We have also chosen walks with refreshments available nearby but it is always wise to take some drinks and nibbles with you – especially if walking with children and dogs – and to check opening times in advance.

Walkers should remember too that the countryside is a changing environment. The walks we have described are as accurate as we can make them but footpaths are sometimes re-routed and changes will inevitably occur over time.
We do hope you will love the Cornish landscape as much as we do.

Happy walking.

BUDE

THE BUDE CANAL. JOURNEY UP THE WEST SIDE OF THE NEET VALLEY TO HELEBRIDGE (PRONOUNCED HEAL BRIDGE) AND BACK ALONG ITS EASTERN SIDE, FOLLOWING THE ROUTE OF THE OLD BUDE TO HOLSWORTHY RAILWAY LINE.

The area of marshy meadows and reed beds which the walk encircles became Cornwall's first nature reserve in 1981 and provides a habitat for numerous wetland birds including reed buntings, willow warblers, moorhens and water rail. Resident ducks, geese and swans tend to congregate around the car park, where they are clearly used to being fed by tourists. Dragonflies are common in summer and, if you are extremely lucky, you just might catch a glimpse of one of the resident otters.

The canal is unusual in that it was designed to carry amphibious 'tub boats'. Instead of using locks, these boats on wheels were hauled, using water power, up a series of six inclined planes with stretches of canal between them.

The canal was built between 1819 and 1825 to carry calcium-rich sand (and some coal) from Bude to inland farming areas stretching to Holsworthy in the east and Launceston to the south. Fifty years later, just as the enterprise was starting to make a profit, the railway arrived and the canal fell into disuse.

The mile-and-a-half stretch of canal in this walk was the only section which could be used

by ordinary canal barges. It has a sea lock, allowing access from the sea at high tide, and two conventional locks which you will pass on the walk.

In 2008 almost £4 million in grant aid was secured to restore the first two miles between the sea lock and the Helebridge incline. These works are now complete and include a wheelchair-friendly towpath and access under the A39.

The return leg is along an equally new and accessible 'multi-use path' along the opposite side of the valley. The first section of the path runs alongside the busy and noisy A39, so we decided to take you on a slightly hillier but prettier alternative route along a very quiet lane through Hele. This does involve crossing the main road but visibility is good and the crossing can be achieved safely under careful supervision.

THE BASICS

Distance: 1, 2 or 3½ miles, 1.6, 3.2 or 5.6 km

Gradient: Mostly level. One very moderate climb on the longer walk

Severity: Easy

Time: ½, 1 or 2 hours

Stiles: None

Map: OS Explorer 111

Path description: Excellent surface – mostly tarmac path

Parking: Bude Crescent (pay) car park (by the TIC). Follow road to town centre from A39. At mini roundabout go straight ahead over river bridge towards Widemouth Bay. Car park will be seen on left. OS Grid Ref. 208062 – EX23 8LE

Landscape: Reedbeds, canal towpath and farmland

Nearest refreshment: The Weir Bistro at Helebridge; Olive Tree Coffee House and Bistro, Bude (by the canal)

BUDE WALK

The Route

1) From the car park, take the canal towpath to the left (away from the bridge) passing a number of converted warehouses on the opposite bank. After 150 yards take the right-hand fork along the towpath. After another 200 yards you will come to a bird hide on the left, which looks over a small  pond and reed beds. Slightly under a half a mile from the car park you will come to a footbridge on the left which, for the one-mile walk, will take you across the River Neet to join the cycle trail next to the rugby field. Turning left onto the trail will bring you back to your starting point.

2) For the longer walks, continue on the towpath for a further half mile to Rodd's Bridge. This is the first bridge over the canal, just past the cast-iron milepost and orange life-saving buoy. For the two-mile walk, turn left at the bridge and follow the lane for 250 yards until you come to the cycle trail where you turn left (just before the dismantled railway bridge) back to the start.

3) For the full-length walk (including one hill and road crossing) cross over Rodd's Bridge and continue on the towpath, which now runs along the right side of the canal. You will pass two locks (neither is in use) and a weir incorporating a fish ladder which was installed to allow sea trout to migrate to their spawning grounds upstream. Eventually, to the right, you will see the fish-stocking lake and the large (and very popular) Weir Bistro on its far bank. Towards the end of the lake you will come to a finger post pointing to Helebridge. Turn left here and keep left on the path which will take you under the A39 and out onto a minor road in Helebridge village. Turn left across two bridges and follow the lane uphill to the small hamlet of Hele.

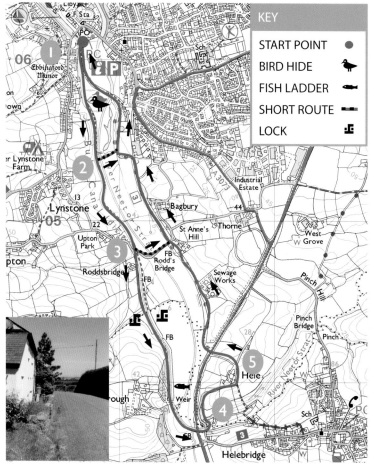

KEY

START POINT	●
BIRD HIDE	🦆
FISH LADDER	🐟
SHORT ROUTE	▬▬
LOCK	⌂

4) At the start of the hill you will pass a small gate onto the A39. This is the official cycle track and will take you alongside the road for 300 yards and then through an underpass. (This avoids the hill, a slightly rough section of path and the road crossing - but is noisy and dull!)

5) Just after the last house in Hele, you will see a path leading down to the main road between high hedges. Follow this path and cross the road with great care (there is a middle island). Continue down the lane opposite, which becomes the multi-use trail, and follow it for the 1½ miles back to the car park. The trail follows the line of the old railway embankment (to the right) and eventually crosses the river on the remains of the old railway bridge.

FLUSHING & MYLOR

THIS EASY (BUT SOMETIMES MUDDY) FOUR-MILE WALK CONNECTS TWO OF THE MAJOR SAILING CENTRES ON THE CARRICK ROADS – REPUTED TO BE THE WORLD'S THIRD LARGEST NATURAL HARBOUR AFTER SYDNEY AND RIO.

We start in the village of Flushing. Once a centre for fishing and boatbuilding, it is now more a dormitory village to Falmouth (a five-minute ferry ride away). The old village is an odd mix of tiny fishermen's cottages and grand sea-captain's mansions and, despite an ever-increasing proportion of second homes, retains a healthy community spirit with its male voice choir, busy sailing and gig-rowing clubs, two good pubs and rowdy regatta week in July/August.

The walk starts with a longish climb through Flushing village and across farmland and

then descends gently through a wooded valley to the edge of Mylor Creek. The creek-side footpath to Mylor takes you past some seriously expensive houses (and their beautiful gardens) and then through an ancient and charming churchyard. It is worth making a short diversion from your route here to the poignant HMS Ganges memorial. The Navy's last sailing flagship, HMS Ganges ended her days off Mylor as a hulk used for training 15- to 17-year-old boys in seamanship.

With a complement of 500, poor sanitation and 'unconventional' methods of discipline, accidents and disease led to the deaths of 53 boys during her stay in Cornwall.

In 1899 the hulk was towed to Suffolk, where HMS Ganges continued as a shore training establishment for the Navy until 1976.

Mylor, once a docking place for packet ships and the wartime base of the French Resistance, is now better known as a busy sailing centre and home to Britain's last remaining fleet of oyster-dredging sailing boats. In 1868 a bylaw was passed restricting oyster dredging in the River Fal to sailing and rowing vessels. As this proved an excellent conservation measure, the law was never rescinded and Falmouth Working Boats can often be seen fishing (or racing) along the next part of your walk.

The final two miles follow the coast path around the Trefusis Estate with views to St Just in Roseland and St Anthony's Head to your left, Pendennis Castle up ahead and the entrance to Falmouth Docks as you round the headland back to Trefusis Beach and Flushing. Many local guides claim the existence of a smugglers' tunnel from the shore at Trefusis Point to a house inland. Our advice is: picture it to yourself – but don't spend too much time looking . . .

THE BASICS

Distance: 4 miles, 6.4km

Gradient: Mostly gentle but with one long climb

Severity: Easy

Time: 2 to 2½ hours

Stiles: Several

Map: OS Explorer 105

Path description: Sometimes muddy paths and field edges

Parking: Follow Trefusis Road through Flushing Village and park on the roadside 100 yards past the sailing club – OS 810336 – TR11 5UB

Landscape: Village, farmland, wood and coastal path

Nearest refreshment: Seven Stars pub or Waterside Restaurant – both on Trefusis Road

The Route

1) If you have parked, as suggested, 100 yards beyond the Sailing Club, continue up Trefusis Road until you see a tarmac path doubling back to your left opposite a large stone house with red brick quoins and a double garage.

   Follow this path up through the recreation area known as the Bowling Green to a small gate leading to a woodland path. Bear left at the bottom of this path, following the narrow lane downhill to a T-junction where you turn right onto Coventry Road. When you reach the end of Coventry Road, turn right onto Kersey Road and walk uphill for 150 yards until you see the entrance to Vinefield Court on your left. Just beyond this entrance you'll find a narrow set of steps on your left leading to an even narrower footpath. Follow the path to the field entrance at its end and then continue uphill keeping the field boundary to your left.

2) At the top of the field (just before the white cottage) you will see a stile in the hedge on your left leading to a gate onto a farm road. Turn left onto this road, over a cattle grid and through a stone gateway to crossroads. Go straight across here (signposted to Mylor Bridge) and, after 50 yards, take the footpath to your right signed Trelew.

3) The path leads downhill through two fields and then becomes a woodland track. Ignoring a fork to the left, follow the track downhill beside a small stream and through large patches of wild garlic (listening for the rattle of woodpeckers!). After passing through a five-bar gate, keep right past a slightly muddy patch of ground and continue along the woodland trail, which leads you over the stream and up some steps to a farm road where you turn right. At the end of this drive, turn right onto a narrow lane keeping the creek on your left. The road ends at a slipway,

   where it narrows to a path leading uphill through an estate (possibly occupied by rock stars and/or city traders?) to the entrance (across a small road) to Mylor churchyard. After entering, but before descending through the churchyard, it is worth diverting a few yards to your left to visit the HMS Ganges memorial.

4) Café, toilets and all the bustle of a busy marina await you in Mylor and, when ready to depart, continue east

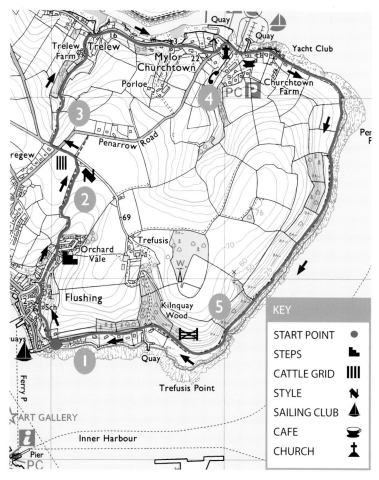

KEY

START POINT	●
STEPS	◣
CATTLE GRID	⦀
STYLE	Ν
SAILING CLUB	⛵
CAFE	☕
CHURCH	✝

along the waterfront (sea on your left) past the sailing club and follow the coast path for approximately two miles around Trefusis Point.

5) As you draw level with the wharves of Falmouth Harbour across the water to your left, the path widens into a broad meadow. At the far end of the meadow in the right-hand corner you will see a hut and five-bar metal gate which will lead you along a track and onto Trefusis Road which, after 400 yards, will return you to your starting point.

LAND'S END

ENGLAND'S MOST WESTERLY POINT, LAND'S END WAS FAMOUSLY THE STARTING POINT FOR THE OLYMPIC TORCH RELAY (AND MANY A CHARITY WALK) AND THE SITE OF BRITAIN'S FIRST AND WORST OIL POLLUTION DISASTER.

It is a windswept and extremely beautiful headland marred, some would say, by an inappropriately large and sprawling visitor centre, but it is nevertheless well worth a visit at any season.

Our walk starts from the visitor centre car park (£5 per car all day when we visited – including entry to the site) and follows the cycle path across heathland to Sennen village, with views across the Longships rocks and lighthouse to the Scilly Isles, just visible on a clear day 25 miles away.

From the end of the cycle track you can complete a short and fairly easy circuit by returning along the coast path, or there is the option to descend into the pretty village to explore the small harbour, lifeboat house, cafés and long sandy beach. The longer walk involves a fairly long descent and the climb back to the cliff path.

Probably the most striking building in Sennen is the Round House, built in the 19th century to house a boat-winching capstan. It is now an art gallery and gift shop. Whitesands Bay consists of a mile of fine sandy beach whose famous canine lifeguard, Bilbo, fell foul of a summer dog ban in 2008!

Above the village you'll pass the disused coastguard lookout with views across Whitesands Bay to the distant mine chimney on Cape Cornwall to the north and the unusual 'Irish Lady' rock (actually, we think, a stone puffin looking out to sea) below you to the south.

Just beyond the puffin are the fast-vanishing remains of the cargo ship RMS Mulheim, which ran aground in 2003. The chief officer on watch caught his trousers on a seat lever and was knocked unconscious in the ensuing fall. All the crew were winched to safety but the ship was wrecked and its cargo of recycled plastic littered local beaches for some years.

Just beyond the wreck, you will pass the remains of an iron-age cliff castle (Maen Castle) and its defensive rampart. Land's End was possibly one of the earliest human settlements in Britain, having escaped the covering of ice which affected the rest of the country and much of Europe.

THE BASICS

Distance: 2 or 2½ miles, 3.2 or 4km

Gradient: Gentle but with one long climb out of the village (longer route)

Severity: Easy

Time: 1 to 1½ hours

Stiles: None

Map: OS Explorer

Path description: Wide cycle track, village and (uneven) coast path

Parking: Land's End visitor centre OS 344250 – TR19 7AA

Landscape: Heath and cliff top

Nearest refreshment: Old Success Inn and the several cafés in Sennen (or various eateries at Land's End visitor centre)

LAND'S END WALK

The Route

1) To the right of the visitor centre (viewed from the car park), you will see two white-painted boulders with arrows to the exit and coach park. Behind the stones (next to the model village) a path leads to the right (towards the car park exit). Follow  this path to its end, where you turn left through a double gate onto the National Cycle Trail. Follow the twists and turns of the cycle trail for one mile (the path follows ancient field boundaries along an impressive granite boulder wall) until it comes to an end at a tarmac road.

2) For the short walk, double back here to your left along a concrete road until, just beyond 'Sharksfin' on your left, you will see a metal gate ahead leading to Maen Cliffs. Follow this track, initially in the direction of the Longships Lighthouse, then curving right to the coastguard lookout (where we will rejoin you presently).

3) For the longer (hillier) walk, continue ahead from the cycle path along the road (between houses) for 250 yards until you come to a wide tarmac path doubling back to your left opposite a house called Pol-an-Dre. This is Stone Chair Lane, and you will pass the stone chair halfway down. You will arrive at the bottom of the hill close to the Round House and just above the small harbour. If you feel like some refreshment, there is a very good little café to the right with outside seating overlooking the sea and the offer of hot water bottles and blankets in cold weather (there is also seating inside)!

4) To continue the walk from the bottom of Stone Chair Lane, you should turn left past the Round House and continue through the car park just above the harbour. At the far end of the car park turn left and take the steps leading up the hillside ahead of you. This is the start of the coast path and will lead you up to the coastguard lookout.

We rejoin the shorter walk here.

5) From the lookout, continue along the coast path for the last ¾ mile to Land's End. As well as the stunning cliff scenery and a profusion of wild flowers in spring, your view will be dominated

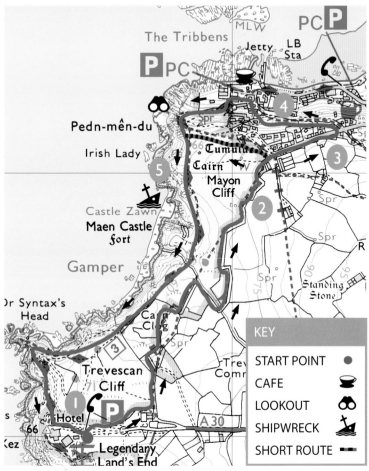

KEY

START POINT	●
CAFE	☕
LOOKOUT	👀
SHIPWRECK	⛵
SHORT ROUTE	▰▰▰

by the 150-year-old Longships Lighthouse. Much of the reef is under water and the many wrecks that lie about it make this a popular destination for divers. Look out, too, for dolphins, basking sharks and gannets, all a common sight along this stretch of coast. Beyond the rock is a busy shipping lane, and if you have the ability and inclination to download the Marine Traffic app to your mobile phone, there is fun to be had checking on the names, destinations and cargoes of passing ships, most of which are now required to broadcast live Automatic Identification Service information.

LANHYDROCK

LANHYDROCK IS ONE OF CORNWALL'S BEST-KNOWN
COUNTRY HOUSES. NOW BELONGING TO THE NATIONAL
TRUST, THE HOUSE AND FORMAL GARDENS ARE WELL
WORTH A VISIT.

The kitchens and fully furnished layout are designed to
show the house as it might have looked in the late Victorian
era. The 1,000 acres of well-tended park and woodland
can be roamed at any time free of charge and the variety of
its delightful (and undemanding) river and woodland trails
tempt us back several times every year.

The current house was largely rebuilt after a fire in the late 19th century with just the North

Wing and Gatehouse surviving from the early 1600s
when the estate was bought and the main house built by
a wealthy Truro merchant called Sir Robert Robartes. His
son John was a prominent supporter of the Roundhead
Army during the Civil War and had to flee to France before
returning to help raise the Royalist siege of Plymouth, as
its Governor.

This fascinating history is related in Daphne du Maurier's
novel The King's General.

The first area of beech and oak woodland you will encounter (the Great Wood) has been
under-planted with an array of rhododendrons, camellias and magnolias as well as
bluebells, primroses and daffodils, so a visit in late April or May will show it at its stunning

best. All the woodland – mostly ancient – is carpeted with wild flowers, mosses and lichens in spring but the walks are lovely at any time of year.

The last part of the walk follows the banks of the River Fowey (two miles above its furthest tidal reach at Lostwithiel) and dogs should be kept on a lead to protect the river bank. The river has seen the successful reintroduction of trout, salmon and a healthy population of otters, and you should look out, too, for dippers (often on rocks in mid-stream) and the blue flash of kingfishers low along the river banks.

The carriage drive described at the start of the walk directions leads (if you were to follow it away from the House) along a pretty riverside trail to Bodmin Parkway Station, so this walk could very well be undertaken using a train connection. The station trail adds just over half a mile in each direction.

The car park at Respryn Bridge (the National Trust asks for a donation via an honesty box) is a little off the beaten track, so you need to consult either a sat-nav or a map or, failing either of these, follow the signs to Lanhydrock and then to Respryn Bridge from there.

THE BASICS

Distance: 2½ miles, 4km

Gradient: Gently sloping or level

Severity: Easy

Time: 1½ hours

Stiles: None

Map: OS Explorer 107, St Austell & Liskeard

Path description: Wide compacted stone and tarmac, well-maintained woodland and river trail

Parking: Respryn Bridge OS 099637 – PL30 4AQ

Landscape: Park and woodland

Dogs: On lead along river bank to protect the banks

Nearest refreshment: Lanhydrock House NT café, Lanhydrock Golf Club or Duchy Nurseries (PL22 0HW)

LANHYDROCK WALK

The Route

1) Exit the car park by the information board, crossing a small wooden bridge to the carriage drive, where you turn left towards Station Lodge. At the lodge gate, cross over the road onto the tarmac drive opposite, which leads uphill to  Newton Lodge. This 1657 lodge house and ornate entrance gateway leads into an impressive beech avenue which was planted to celebrate the Parliamentary Army's victory in the English Civil War. Several of the original sycamores are said to survive.

2) Continue up the avenue until you reach the ornate gatehouse at Lanhydrock, where you turn left and follow the garden wall (on the outside). Just before you arrive at the stable entrance (leading to the café, shop and toilets), you take the gate on your left leading into the Great Wood.

Continue ahead on the wide uphill track through a magnificent plantation of rhododendrons and camellias (ignoring an early branch off to the left (Lady's Walk)). As the path levels out at the top of the hill, follow the main track as it curves to the right and ignore the slightly narrower paths leading to left and right. This will lead you past Garden Cottage and the walled kitchen gardens (and poly-tunnels) on your left. Beyond the walled garden, the track continues straight ahead with wide views across the Fowey Valley and then downhill to the left through another woodland plantation.

4) Follow the main path as it curves away downhill to the right, now with a low stone wall on its left side. At the end of the low wall, take the path doubling back to your left where a finger post directs you to Respryn River Walks. This takes you along a wooded valley (Maudlin Wood) with a stream on your right to a wooden farm gate at its end. Follow the track past two fields to a second gate, beyond which you take the path downhill to your right signposted to 'Respryn via Footbridge'. Continue straight on downhill through another (red) gate (ignore the field entrance to your right) until you reach the Fowey River.

5) Turn left along the river path with the river on your right, past the little arch and

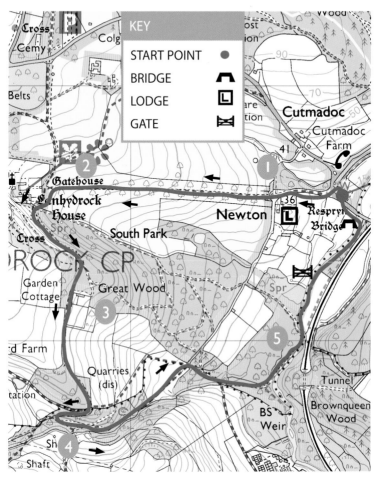

KEY

START POINT ●
BRIDGE
LODGE Ⓛ
GATE

railway sign telling you that you are 275 miles and 10 chains from Paddington Station on the Great Western Main Line!

When you reach the footbridge, cross the river and continue along the opposite bank until you reach the beautiful stone road bridge at Respryn. Cross the bridge and you will see your car park starting point to the right.

LERRYN

LYING AT THE CENTRE OF A MAZE OF NARROW LANES
BETWEEN FOWEY AND POLPERRO, LERRYN IS A BACKWATER
THAT IS REALLY WORTH DISCOVERING.

The now sleepy village was once an important trading centre thanks to its 16th-century bridge and accessibility by boat from the coast. This trade gradually ceased as the River Fowey became badly silted by mining waste from Bodmin Moor.

Silver was smelted here in the reign of Elizabeth I, and the brooding woodland on the south bank of the river is said to have been the inspiration for Kenneth Graham's 'Wild Wood' in The Wind in the Willows.

Until the early 20th century, the woodlands along the Lerryn River provided employment for rinders – who would cut oak bark every May for the tannery at Grampound – and for firewood cutters who would supply the many cloam ovens then in use, as well as timber for hurdles and wheel spokes.

At the juncture of the Fowey and Lerryn rivers you will glimpse, on the far bank of the Fowey, the black and white Penquite Boathouse. This was the point at which Garibaldi probably landed in 1864 (he stayed at Penquite House – latterly Golant Youth Hostel).

The boathouse was built some 30 years later and was visited by the Prince of Wales (later

Edward VII) who, according to a plaque on the building, 'besported himself with young ladies'! Look out also for little egrets (a pure white heron which has recently become common in parts of south Cornwall) and kingfishers flying low along the water's edge.

The longer of our two walks takes in the even sleepier hamlet of St Winnow whose tranquillity, save for the odd barking farm dog and the ringing of church bells on a Sunday morning, surely cannot be equalled anywhere in England. Much remains of its 15th-century church including font, rood screens, bench-end carvings and stained glass, so do take some time here.

Home-made cream teas and filled rolls are available in summer from Angie's mobile café – also not to be missed.

Climbing the hill from St Winnow, stop now and again to enjoy the panorama behind you with St Winnow nestling below and Penquite House on the far bank of the river.

THE BASICS

Distance: 2 miles or 4½ miles via St Winnow) 3.2 or 7.2km

Gradient: One steep ascent on the longer walk

Severity: Easy

Time: 1 (or 2½) hour(s)

Stiles: None on short walk but many on longer route

Map: OS Explorer 107, St Austell & Liskeard

Path description: Half a mile across (sometimes muddy) fields on longer route. Otherwise well-defined paths

Parking: Public (free) car park (occasionally floods at spring tides). OS 140570 – PL22 0PT

Landscape: Woodland, tidal river, farmland

Nearest refreshment: Ship Inn at start/end of walk

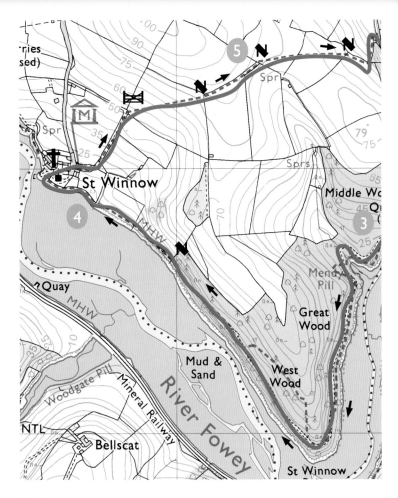

The Route

1) Except at high tide (or if it's not your thing!) the walk starts by crossing the river by stepping stones from the car park. The alternative is to cross by the ancient bridge and follow the roads around to the left until you reach the opposite bank.

   Follow the creek-side path (river on your left) past a handful of cottages and a converted granary and into Ethy Wood.

2) Continue along the river path for half a mile. Just past an ancient granite post the path turns right at a spot called Ethy Rock. This was once a wharf and is a popular picnic spot. After a further 200 yards the path divides and you should take the left fork across some stepping stones and a small wooden bridge (a good place to

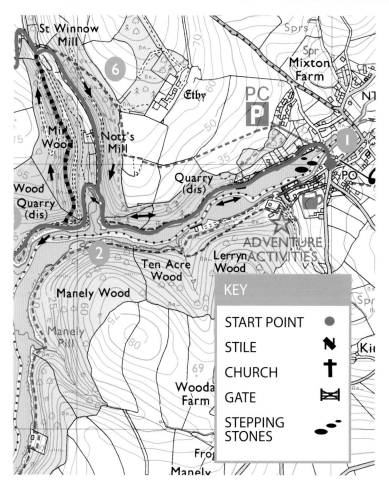

KEY

START POINT	●
STILE	N
CHURCH	†
GATE	⋈
STEPPING STONES	⬝⬝⬝

play 'Pooh sticks' if you have children) and climb gently for a few hundred yards until you reach a wide forestry track.

For the shorter walk, turn right here and follow the forest track for a third of a mile until you reach a pole barrier across the track and the ruined St Winnow Mill on your right. Turn right past the mill to rejoin the longer walk.

3) For the longer walk, turn left on the forestry track and continue for 1½ miles with the river and ancient woodland still on your left and a Forestry Commission plantation on your right. After ¾ mile the track bends to the right as the River Lerryn joins the larger River Fowey. A bench has been thoughtfully located to afford you a stunning view down the river to Golant on your right and

Fowey's china clay docks in the far distance. The forest track ends at a stile leading to open farmland. Continue along the bottom edge of two fields to the foreshore below St Winnow church. Follow the shoreline until you reach a small boathouse (now a holiday cottage) on your right. Follow the lane to the right past an ancient farmhouse, to the church entrance.

4) From the church head up the road for 30 yards and take the signed public footpath on your right. Follow the fairly rough track for about 200 yards, ending with gates into three fields and a track off to your left. The gate ahead and to your right is the one you want, with a stile and public footpath arrow. Continue uphill across a large field to the five-bar gate at the top.

5) On reaching the gate, cross the two stiles and continue across the next field with the hedge on your left. At the end of this field bear right across a field towards the next farm gate and stile which are marked with a yellow post. Cross the stile and continue in the same direction to the lower far corner of the next field (again marked with a yellow post and stile). Follow the hedge on your left to a further stile and then downhill through a final field (with the hedge on your right) until you pass a slate-clad cottage. Here a stile will lead you onto an unmetalled road. Turn right onto the road, and almost immediately bear left past the ruins of St Winnow Mill.

Those of you on the shorter walk rejoin us here.

6) Follow the mainly level path along the valley side, ignoring a turning to Nott's Mill on your right, and after a third of a mile you will find yourself back at Ethy Rock. Retrace your steps back along the river path to the stepping stones.

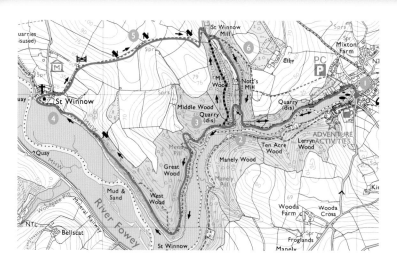

LIZARD

Though popular with tourists, the Lizard remains largely unspoilt and offers an easily accessible glimpse of one of Cornwall's wildest and most beautiful stretches of coastline.

The geology is unique in Britain, consisting of oceanic, green serpentine rock which is easily recognisable along the paths as it becomes polished by the constant foot traffic. Souvenir shops in the village sell turned serpentine lamps and lighthouses.

No fewer than twelve rights of way radiate from Lizard Village Green to points around the Lizard headland, from Kynance Cove on the western side around to Church Cove in the east. It is therefore easily possible to extend your walk to six miles or reduce it to under two. We have classified the walk as moderate as there are several quite steep flights of steps and one biggish hill, but the majority of the walking is easy along good paths.

Well known as Britain's most southerly point, the Lizard is also famous as the re-established home (since 2002) of Cornwall's iconic but long-absent chough (an acrobatic, red-legged crow), and notorious for the numerous ships wrecked on its shores and outlying reefs.

The old lifeboat station on Lizard Point carried out 136 rescues between 1859 and 1961

(when it was moved a mile to the east to the more sheltered Kilcobben Cove), saving 562 lives. Probably its most famous rescue (the RNLI's biggest of all time) was of the White Star liner SS Suevic, which went aground on the Point on her way home from Australia in 1907. All her 382 passengers survived thanks to the bravery of four local lifeboat crews in high seas, fog and darkness.

Those choosing to extend their walk to the new lifeboat station (an extra mile along the coast path) will pass the old Lloyds signal station, built in 1872 so that ships entering and leaving the channel could send messages by semaphore to be relayed by telegraph to the ships' owners.

Just beyond the signal station are two small huts (now a museum maintained by the National Trust) where Guglielmo Marconi undertook his earliest long-distance wireless telegraphy experiments.

Look out for seals around Lizard Point and for the pink and yellow succulent, the hottentot fig, an invader from South Africa which has colonised large areas of cliff to the displeasure of conservationists.

THE BASICS

Distance: 2½ miles (3½ via Lifeboat Station) 4 or 5.6km
Gradient: Mainly gentle gradients but one tough climb
Severity: Moderate
Time: 1¼ hours (1¾ hours via Lifeboat Station)
Stiles: None
Map: OS Explorer 103, The Lizard
Path description: Coast path; village roads
Parking: Lizard Village Green car park (donations), OS 703125 – TR12 7NQ
Landscape: Village lanes, coast path and grazing enclosures
Nearest refreshments: Pubs and cafés in the village and cafés on Lizard Point

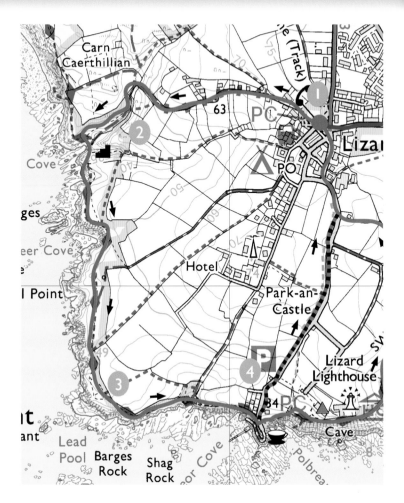

The Route

1) From the village green, take the tarmac lane to the right of the toilet block (signposted Caerthillian and Kynance Coves), passing between the 'no through road' and 'turning area' signs and past a stall sometimes selling home-made jam.

   Follow the lane to its end (ignoring the right turn to Kynance Cove unless you are opting for the very longest walk). You might see the two charming Shetland ponies whom we stopped to chat to in a field to your left.

2) At Porthbean House the lane becomes a footpath which you follow past an information board, through tamarisk and blackthorn thickets, over a small stream and downhill to join the coast path at Caerthillian Cove.

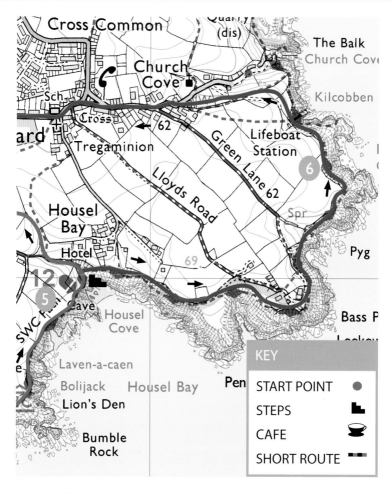

Turn left on the coast path across a stream and up a flight of steps and a longish climb. The path becomes more gently sloping through an amazing array of wild flowers in spring and with breathtaking views along the coast in both directions. The path is grazed in winter by ponies and cattle, who are part of a scheme to encourage the spread of wild flowers and to provide a habitat for the nesting choughs.

3) The path turns left to reveal Britain's most southerly point. Look out for choughs along the cliffs to your right or over the stone walls to your left, where they may sometimes be seen feeding.

4) I doubt if there can be a more spectacular setting in Britain for coffee or lunch

than on the terrace of the 'Most Southerly Café' at Lizard Point. A tame jackdaw perched next to our table, evidently expecting a few crumbs.

You have the option to follow the road the third of a mile back to Lizard Village from here (a good footpath runs alongside the road most of the way) if you wish to avoid the final steep section at Housel Bay.

Otherwise, continue east on the coast path from Lizard Point car park for just over half a mile, passing the 18th-century lighthouse with its two enormous black foghorns. Across Housel Bay you will see the former Lloyds signal station (square white building) with Bass Point Coastwatch Station to its right. The path comes close to the cliff edge just above Housel beach and, if you have a good head for heights, you may wish to look for fulmar and jackdaw nests on the cliffs.

5) Just before you reach the Housel Bay Hotel you negotiate a steep flight of steps down and back up again, at which point you should leave the coast path and follow the blue arrow ahead of you signed Lizard Village.

Those opting for the longer walk should continue on the coast path (a further mile) to the lifeboat station, where you then follow the access road back to the village centre.

6) Cross the road at the top of the path and turn right up a gravel track until it rejoins the road again after 200 yards. Ignore the footpath opposite and follow the road uphill, leaving the thatched cottage to your left and Serpentine Works to your right until you arrive back at the village green.

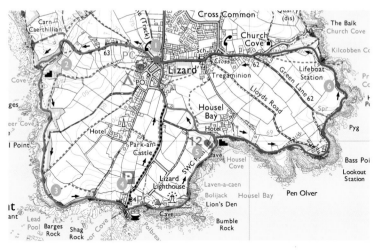

LOE POOL

Described as 'one of Cornwall's glorious surprises', this trail combines the tranquil enjoyment of lakeside paths with one of south Cornwall's most exposed and dangerous stretches of beach.

The walk takes you close to Porthleven so there is the opportunity to explore this traditional fishing village and/ or refresh yourselves at one of its many excellent pubs and cafés.

Cornwall's largest freshwater lake, Loe Pool was once a tidal estuary, but just when and how it became separated from the sea by the sand and shingle bank at Loe Bar is still hotly contested by mythologists and geographers.

One popular myth has it that a giant dropped his bag of sand across the estuary whilst running from another giant who was hurling rocks at him (one missed and landed in the sea to become St Michael's Mount).

Another says that it was dropped from a sack by the ghost of a Bodmin Magistrate called Tregeagle who had been given the impossible task (amongst others) of moving the beach at Gunwalloe to Porthleven whilst being pursued relentlessly by the devil's hell-hounds. The bag theory is questioned by some geographers, however, who claim it is more likely to have resulted from glacial activity at the end of the last ice age or, more recently, from longshore drift.

What is definitely known is that the lake's ability to drain to the sea was all but lost in the 18th and 19th centuries as the shingle bar became clogged with mine waste. This has periodically resulted in serious flooding upstream at Helston (most recently in 2012), necessitating the cutting of a channel to the sea (pumping seems now to be the preferred option).

Legend also has it that King Arthur's sword, 'Excalibur', was cast into Loe Pool by Sir Bedivere as Arthur lay dying, and was taken by a hand which rose out of the lake. Tennyson is said to have had Loe Bar in mind when he described 'a dark strait of barren land. / On one side lay the Ocean, and on one / Lay a great water, and the moon was full.' in his poem 'Morte d'Arthur'.

There is also a belief locally that Loe claims a victim every seven years. There have certainly been many shipwrecks along the strand and the beach is signed as unsafe for swimming due to a powerful undertow.

On a lighter note, it is worth bringing a pair of binoculars as you are likely to see many species of duck, including teal and widgeon, and don't forget to look up as well for the cormorants that roost in the tall trees around the water's edge.

The final surprise in store for you on this interesting short walk will be the discovery of a series of 'green gyms' along the woodland trail. Logs have been imaginatively adapted to provide a variety of exercise aids!

THE BASICS

Distance: 3 miles 4.8km

Gradient: Mainly level or gently sloping

Severity: Easy

Time: 1½ hours

Stiles: None – one flight of steps down

Map: OS Explorer 103, The Lizard

Path description: Woodland trail; coast path; minor roads

Parking: Penrose Hill car park (free). Turn left off the B3304 (Helston to Porthleven) signed to Loe Bar. After 50 yards, turn left at the thatched (Whitstone) cottage OS 639258 – TR13 0RB

Landscape: Lakeside woodland; coastal slope; farmland

Nearest refreshment: Pubs and cafés in Porthleven Village (none on route)

LOE POOL WALK

The Route

1) Take the path at the bottom left corner of the car park, across the estate drive (next to an information board) and continue down the woodland path, soon rejoining the estate road that you crossed earlier. At the crossroads, turn right following the sign to Helston and Loe Bar, bearing left after a short distance towards an ornate stone bridge. The Bath House to your left was built in 1837 by the then estate owner in mock Roman style (the bridge was built ten years later).

2) Some 250 yards beyond the bridge, turn right following the sign to Loe Bar. You should now see Penrose House to your right. (Loe Pool and several miles of foreshore were gifted to the National Trust in 1975 with the condition that it should be maintained as a place of great beauty for people to enjoy without distraction. Boating, swimming and fishing are not allowed.)

3) Follow the path around past the coach house and up a gentle incline with the lake and railings to your left. The path follows the lakeside for about a mile and you will shortly come across the first of the series of green gyms. The woodland is predominantly beech and oak with carpets of bluebells, primroses and pink campion in April and early May.

4) The track ends at the Lodge at Loe Bar where it merges with the coast path, with sweeping views to the Lizard and Land's End peninsulas. Follow the coast path now towards Porthleven (keep the sea on your left) for ¾ mile. Swimming is particularly hazardous at Loe Bar as there is a hidden shelf just below the low tide line and a reef beyond it. In 1807, 190 sailors were drowned when the frigate HMS Anson tried to beach on the bar in a gale. A local man, Henry Trengrouse, witnessed the disaster and was inspired to invent a musket- mounted, rocket-propelled lifeline. Rocket apparatus has since been credited with saving more than 5,000 lives.

5) The coastpath ends with a flight of steps down to a small car park. Follow the road up past a row of holiday cottages to its end where you turn right just past an imposing stone house (once home to actress Jenny Agutter) and continue uphill for ¼ mile. Turn

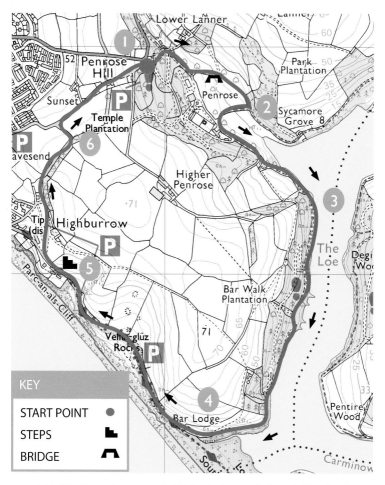

right at the T-junction onto a slightly busier lane and after a further ¼ mile you will see the thatched cottage on your right, where you entered the car park.

LUXULYAN VALLEY

BARELY A STONE'S THROW FROM THE URBAN
CONGLOMERATION OF ST AUSTELL, PAR AND ST BLAZEY
LIES ONE OF THE MOST BEAUTIFUL, PEACEFUL AND
ARCHEOLOGICALLY IMPORTANT VALLEYS IN CORNWALL.

Hidden down the tiniest of country lanes, the Luxulyan (pronounced 'luxillion') Valley was, in the mid to late 19th century, at the heart of one of the county's most important and ambitious mining and quarrying enterprises.

Ghosts are everywhere amongst the overgrown industrial remains of leats, tramways, sluices and waterwheels and along the magnificent Treffry Aqueduct, whose ten arches soar 100 feet above the valley floor. The viaduct, tramway and an incline climbing 300 feet from Ponts Mill were built in the 1840s by Joseph Treffry to ship granite, ore and china clay from the high ground to the north-west to his newly constructed harbour at Par. The leats also served the important Fowey Consols copper mines.

Despite the construction of a mineral railway along the valley bottom in 1874 the viaduct remained in commercial use until 1933. It still carries water to a small hydro-electric plant at Ponts Mill and is probably the most spectacular 200 yards of inland footpath in Cornwall.

The Wheelpit Mill (the remains of which you'll pass on this walk) originally comprised a 30-foot waterwheel to pull carts up the Carmears incline. It was later enlarged and adapted to grind china stone for porcelain manufacture. (The Friends of Luxulyan Valley have produced an excellent website (www.luxulyanvalley.co.uk) giving far more information about the valley's fascinating history, flora and fauna than we have room for here)

Some 300 years ago the sea reached almost to Ponts Mill before receding the two miles to Par due to silting from mine waste. The mill was once the first crossing point on what was then an estuary and ships of up to 80 tons moored here in the 18th century.

The walk starts from Ponts Mill and follows the route of the first tramway built along the valley floor beside the fast-flowing River Par. Once badly polluted, the river now supports a healthy fish population as well as dippers (which we saw) and otters (which we didn't!). You'll pass the ruins of a 20th-century clay dry where china clay slurry was dried to a powder by coal furnaces. Children (closely supervised) will enjoy exploring these remains as the access walkways, ovens and settling tanks have all been made accessible.

You'll soon start to notice the enormous granite boulders which litter the landscape and river bank. Created by subterranean chemical weathering, they include 'Big Rock' – the largest free-standing granite boulder in Europe – weighing in excess of 1,200 tons.

You'll pass under the Treffry Viaduct and up a woodland path to its eastern end. From there you'll follow the upper tramway to Wheelpit Mill and end with a long descent down the incline to your starting point.

THE BASICS

Distance: 2½ miles, 4km

Gradient: Long slopes but mainly gentle gradients

Severity: Easy

Time: 1½ hours

Stiles: None but some steps

Map: OS Explorer 107, St Austell & Liskeard

Path description: Well-maintained woodland trails

Parking: Ponts Mill (free) car park OS 073562 – PL24 2RR. Leaving St Blazey eastbound on the A390, turn left to Ponts Mill at a very minor crossroads half a mile past the level crossing. Follow this narrow lane to the car park at its end

Landscape: Wooded valley and hillside

Nearest refreshment: Several pubs on the A390 through Par

LUXULYAN VALLEY WALK

The Route

1) As you enter the car park, the cycle track leading to the Luxulyan Valley will be seen to your right, just beyond a stone parapet.  Follow this track, beneath the electricity lines (which serve the hydro-electric turbine house), to a gate and information board. Beyond the gate, the cycle track leads you steadily up the valley, passing beneath the railway viaduct, past the ruined Trevanney Clay Dry (in use until 1965), crossing the river at two points and finally crossing beneath the Par to Newquay railway line a second time.

   Some 200 yards beyond this second crossing, follow the path uphill as it turns right away from the river. A little further on you will pass one of the valley's huge boulders to your right and catch your first glimpse of the soaring arches of the Treffry Viaduct through the tree tops.

2) Follow the path under the arches until you reach a small clearing with an information board just before the little car park. Turn right here up some steps and immediately right again alongside the leat. After 20 yards, cross the wooden bridge and follow the woodland path uphill to the south-east end of the viaduct.

3) The tramway you will be following from here leads directly away from the viaduct but, before starting back on the 'high road' to Ponts Mill, you will be well rewarded (provided you've a good head for heights) by a short sortie across the viaduct and back.

4) Now take the tramway away from the viaduct as it follows the higher leat for just over half a mile to the Wheel Pit at the  top of Carmears incline. Look out for the boundary stone on the left of the path with a T (for Treffry) on one side and a K (for his neighbour, Kendall) on the other.

5) When you reach the Wheel Pit (with the smithy on your left), you will shortly be starting on the long descent down the incline (leaving the ruined checker's cabin to your right). There is the option here to take a short diversion down the steps to one or other side of the old mill. If you

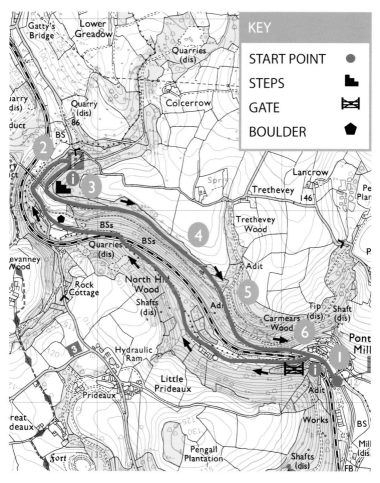

KEY

START POINT ●

STEPS ▪

GATE ⬌

BOULDER ⬟

take this route, turn left on reaching the path below the mill and then right onto the incline after a few yards.

6) You'll pass under a stone bridge which carried a carriage drive connecting Pelyn House with the church at Luxulyan (later renamed the 'velvet path' as it became overgrown with moss).

At the foot of the incline, pass through the gate ahead back to your starting point.

MINIONS

Cornwall's highest village was built on virgin moorland in the 1860s and 70s to serve the quarrying, mining and railway activities which reached a peak at around that time.

Tin mining on Minions Moor has taken place since the Bronze Age and its well-preserved stone circles testify to its importance at around 1500 BC. The moor around Minions village is pockmarked with excavations from the Middle Ages and mineshafts (many still uncapped) from the 18th and 19th centuries.

By the late 19th century the area would have been an industrial wasteland, noisy and polluting, sending thousands of tons of crushed waste into the Fowey and Looe estuaries and encouraging the spread of lawless shanty settlements as miners and their families moved onto the moor from West Cornwall.

Now ferns and moss have returned and the 50 or more remaining mine buildings are picturesque ruins; the granite sleepers along the once busy railway lines are a romantic echo from an era of high hopes, technical innovations, lost fortunes and hard, short lives. This short walk perhaps encapsulates the spirit and character of Bodmin Moor better than any other. It begins at the impressive Hurlers stone circles, thought from their celestial alignment to be mid Bronze Age but said locally to be the petrified remains of participants in a game of hurling (a no-holds-barred sport still played in parts of Cornwall) which had unwisely been scheduled on the Sabbath!

We then follow a good but uneven stone cart track to the Cheesewring – an improbably shaped outcrop of granite on a small tor, believed to have achieved its unusual shape (in common with similar outcrops across Bodmin Moor and Dartmoor) from millions of years of weathering (other theories are available!).

The scramble up to the summit of the tor is, of course, optional but the views from the top on a fine day are of a kind which will never be captured on a camera. The circle back to Minions is completed along the disused quarry line, stopping at a visitor centre housed in the former Houseman's engine house (part of the South Phoenix mine complex which closed in the early 20th century). There is much to be said of this small area of moorland which can't be detailed in this limited space, and it is worth allowing yourself time to enjoy this excellent resource.

THE BASICS

Distance: 2 miles, 3.2km

Gradient: Level or gently sloping with quite a steep scramble up the tor (optional)

Severity: Easy

Time: 1½ hours

Stiles: None

Map: OS Explorer 109, Bodmin Moor

Path description: Cropped moorland, uneven stone track

Parking: Follow signs to Minions from A38 at Doublebois. Hurlers car park is on left at entrance to village. OS 260712 – PL14 5LW

Landscape: Exposed moorland

Dogs: Must be kept under close supervision as there are sheep, cattle and ponies grazing and open mineshafts are a hazard

Nearest refreshment: Cheesewring Hotel, Hurlers Halt & Minion Tea Rooms in village

MINIONS WALK

The Route

1) Steps and a metal rail lead up from the top left-hand end of the car park to a stone cart track. Turn right onto this track, which leads directly away from the road in a north-easterly direction.

2) You should immediately see the two main stone circles to your right and you will probably wish to wander in their direction to mingle with the stones and watch the ponies. Return to the cart track once you have finished mingling. Continue on the cart track for approximately ¾ mile, ignoring a fork off to your left. You will pass two standing stones to your right. Apparently these 'Pipers' also made the mistake of playing on the Sabbath. We also passed a herd of Belted Galloway cattle which is one of a number of unusual breeds suited to moorland living.

3) When the track splits into three (just past an enormous concrete-filled tyre at the time of writing) take the right-hand of the three tracks, which will lead you down across a little valley. As you climb out of the valley, follow the track as it curves up and to the right with a series of fenced-off mineshafts to your right and the Cheesewring ahead and to your left .

4) Close to the foot of the tor, you will come to a crossroads in the path. To continue the walk, you should follow the path straight ahead with a deep ditch to your left. To explore the Cheesewring, however, turn left at the crossroads and take one of a number of small paths which lead up to a barbed-wire fence which protects people (but not dogs) from a deep quarry beyond. Turn left along the fence and follow the path to the top. Near the foot of this climb, look for the remains of the 18th century cave home of the stone cutter Daniel Gumb. Although often referred to as a hermit, he reputedly shared the cave with two (successive) wives, Thomazine and Florence. He is said to have been an amateur astronomer and philosopher and some of his geometric drawings are still visible on a nearby stone.

5) Once back at the crossroads, follow the path beside the ditch which curves left around the quarry before turning to the right and following the old railway track bed in the direction of the Caradon Hill TV mast.

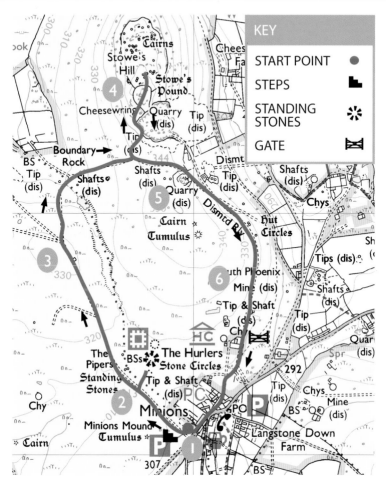

KEY

START POINT	●
STEPS	◣
STANDING STONES	✳
GATE	⊠

6) The old tramway leads in a gentle curve to the right around the hill and ends at a gate with the South Phoenix engine house and visitor centre to your right. On leaving the engine house, follow the track into the village (ignoring a turn to the

left into a car park). This brings you onto the road by the Cheesewring pub (toilets here on the right). Turn right onto the road and the car park from which you started will be found on the right after a short distance.

MORWENSTOW

Despite its size, there is something very special about Morwenstow, with its eccentric parson and ramshackle hut on the cliffs.

Surrounded by organic farmland and set close to the high cliffs and unforgiving rocky shore of Cornwall's most northerly stretch of coast, the hamlet is dominated by its Norman church (the font is believed to be 10th century) with its ancient carved bench ends and a window dedicated to Parson Hawker (and his dog), the parish's vicar from 1834 to 1874.

Claims made about Parson Hawker's numerous foibles may have been embellished over time and include his dressing as a mermaid and combing his hair on rocks below the cliffs, excommunicating a cat for mousing on Sundays (his nine cats and pet pig were said to have attended church) and conversing with birds. What is not disputed is that he introduced harvest festivals to the church calendar, defied convention by burying drowned sailors in his churchyard (there are 40 such graves including the captain and crew of the Caledonian – its figurehead can be seen in the church), built a hut on the cliffs from driftwood where he would meditate and write poetry (Lord Tennyson is said to have been a visitor) and that he wrote Cornwall's well-known anthem, 'Trelawny' ('The Song of the Western Men'). Hawker's Hut is now the National Trust's smallest property and can be visited on the walk.

Below the church is the large rectory built by Parson Hawker with chimney stacks depicting various churches and an Oxford College with which he had been associated. This very short, mainly level walk starts from the parking area above the church, takes you through the churchyard and across three small fields to the cliffs, south along the

cliff top to Hawker's Hut and then back along a farm lane past the Bush Inn, a friendly 13th-century free house, and along the very minor road back up to the glebe. Next to the parking area are the (also 13th-century) Rectory Farm Tea Rooms. There is seating inside and out and a menu featuring locally sourced and home-grown food including gluten- and dairy-free options.

The walk can be easily extended either by following the footpath past the rectory and along the valley side to Henna Cliff or by continuing south from Hawker's Hut to Higher Sharpnose Point and back along the valley to the south of Morwenstow.

BUT . . . in either case strenuous climbs and/or descents are involved!

THE BASICS

Distance: 1½ miles, 2.4km. Longer route approx 3 miles, 5km

Gradient: Mainly level or gently sloping

Severity: Easy

Time: 1 hour

Stiles: One – from church. This can be avoided by taking the short lane above the church

Map: OS Explorer 126, Clovelly & Hartland

Path description: Field boundary, coast path, farm access track and minor road

Parking: Follow signs to Morwenstow from A39 and continue to the end of the road. OS 206153 – EX23 9SR (takes you to the Bush Inn but keep going!)

Landscape: Grazed farmland, dramatic cliff top

Nearest food: Bush Inn and Rectory Farm Tearooms (daily from late March)

MORWENSTOW WALK

The Route

1) Enter the churchyard through the lychgate. A little exploring is recommended before visiting the ancient church. Ahead and to your left you will see a replica of the Caledonia's white figurehead which marks the grave of the ship's crew – the restored original is now inside the church. From the bottom right-hand corner of the churchyard a public path leads beside a wall towards the rectory. Without being intrusive, you may wish to follow this for a few yards to get a better view of the rectory chimneys.

2) Turn right out of the church door and follow the path to a stile leading into a grass field. Follow the left-hand edge of this and the next two paddocks until you reach the coast path, where you turn left.

3) Follow the cliff-top path southwards for 200 yards until you reach the entrance to a short path leading down to Hawker's Hut. The hut is extremely picturesque and the views from it are breathtaking. To your left is Higher Sharpnose Point and below you Vicarage Cliffs, both popular with climbers. There are said to be kestrels and peregrines nesting in the area and grey seals are common along this coast, so keep your eyes skinned.

Just before you rejoin the footpath, look for a cache on your left where a variety of strange objects and a book for visitors' comments have been secreted. Amazingly, given the exposed location, comments dating back four years were legible when we visited.

Turn right onto the coast path and continue to the next kissing gate (approx 50 yards). Immediately past the gate a path runs inland to your left and this is the one you should take for our short (easy) walk. You may wish to continue ahead to the top of a steep descent where you can assess the longer route which takes you to the Bush Inn via the partly wooded Tidna Valley with an optional (and very vertiginous) excursion along the ridge of Higher Sharpnose Point.

4) Our easy route takes you along the left-hand edge of two grazed fields, through a couple more kissing gates and onto a stone farm track between two Cornish hedges. We have walked this route on two successive summers and on each

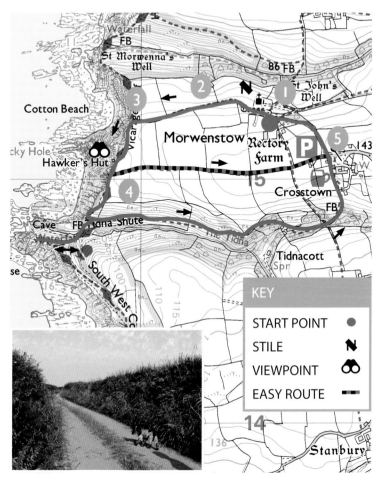

KEY

START POINT	●
STILE	N
VIEWPOINT	👀
EASY ROUTE	▬▬

occasion there has been a profusion of butterflies (mostly cabbage whites but with some more exotic species) along this track.

5) The track ends at the road next to the Bush Inn, where you turn left and follow the lane for 250 yards back to the parking area. You will pass on your left an entrance to Aunt Amy's garden, which was until recently a charming oasis where you were invited to sit and rest. Alas nature has taken over – but who knows when the local WI may revisit with strimmers and secateurs . . .

MOUNT EDGCUMBE

THE 865 ACRES OF CORNWALL'S EARLIEST LANDSCAPED
PARK WERE BOUGHT FROM THE EDGCUMBE ESTATE IN 1971
BY CORNWALL AND PLYMOUTH CITY COUNCILS.

The main park, including its Grade I listed gardens, is open throughout the year free of charge. The Tudor mansion, rebuilt from a ruin after having been bombed during World War II, opens on Sundays to Thursdays between April and September (full details at www.mountedgcumbe.gov.uk).

The park occupies the toe of the boot-shaped Rame Peninsula (Cornwall's south-eastern extremity), jutting out into Plymouth Sound with panoramic views on three sides to the Tamar bridges, Devonport dockyards, Plymouth, Drake's Island, and around to Cawsand and Rame Head.

Occupying such a prominent position at the entrance to one of England's most important naval bases, it is not surprising that the house and its land were involved in several military adventures: a battle took place here during the Civil War and in 1779 a fleet of 80 French and Spanish ships anchored close by in preparation for an intended invasion. In 1944, Mount Edgcumbe was the D-Day embarkation point for part of the US Army's 29th Infantry Division. Most of the concrete roads you will encounter date from this period.

The walk takes you past the 21-gun Garden Battery – constructed in 1741 to salute ships (other than French or Spanish!) entering the harbour (just three of the cannon remain) – and along Barn Pool, which was used as an anchorage by Vikings in 997.

The park includes Britain's National Camellia Collection, with over 1,000 cultivars, and visitors are invited to follow a waymarked Camellia Trail (not part of this walk) from January

through to April. The formal gardens, planted around 200 years ago in the English, French, Italian and, more recently, American and New Zealand styles occupy the lower part of the park. It is well worth setting aside 15 or 30 minutes to wander amongst these beautiful and peaceful gardens when you reach the Orangery tea rooms.

There is a foot passenger ferry from Plymouth to Cremyll – the small village at the lower entrance to the park – and if you arrive by this means you will need to pick up the route from the Lower Park entrance (following signs to the Orangery).

THE BASICS

Distance: 3 miles, 4.8km

Gradient: Two challenging flights of steps and some moderate hills

Severity: First half easy – second half moderate with two long flights of steps

Time: 2 hours

Stiles: None

Map: OS Explorer 108, Lower Tamar Valley & Plymouth

Path description: Grass parkland, coast path and well-made trails

Parking: Upper Car Park, Mount Edgcumbe Country Park, nr Maker Church OS 447520 – PL10 1HZ Sat-nav will take you too far so look out for church and stone cross (or public pay car park in Cremyll just to explore the gardens and lower park)

Landscape: Parkland; woodland; coast

Nearest refreshment: Orangery and Stables in the park (seasonal); Edgcumbe Arms pub in Cremyll

MOUNT EDGCUMBE WALK

The Route

1) The upper car park next to Maker Church is approached through an impressive gateway next to a large stone cross on the right of the road.

   Starting from the gate next to the animal pens and a wooden structure, set off across the deer park (away from the church), with views to Plymouth and the Tamar to your left. After 50 yards the path splits and you should take the left fork, leading downhill to a gate into an area of bluebell woods.

2) Follow the woodland path to an estate road where you turn right past a car park on your left. Ignore a spur to your right and continue downhill to a staggered crossroads where you turn left, signed to the Orangery. (The path to the right at the crossroads is the start of the Camellia Trail).

3) Follow the roadway downhill, ignoring turnings to left and right, past a duck pond and through an avenue of trees taking you away from the big house and towards the ferry slipway and Lower Park entrance. Turn right here to the Orangery.

4) You should pick up the walk at this point if you arrived by ferry or parked in the Cremyll car park.

   Pass through the arched passage into the formal gardens, skirting around the Orangery (to your left), then between high hedges to the waterfront path with views to Devil's Point and the Mayflower Marina. (The gardens can be accessed by turning right at the Orangery past the fountain.)

5) Keep left along the waterfront past the Blockhouse, Garden Battery and Barn Pool Beach and through a stretch of woodland, passing a small lake on your right and keeping straight ahead across the grass to the Doric Temple. The coast path becomes narrower and rougher here and you are warned about 'dangerous cliffs and paths'.

6) Continue through woodland to a tall wooden gate below the Folly (intended as a 'ruin' in 1747 – the Earl had his workers build it and then blew it up to achieve the desired effect!). Pass through the gate and continue ahead, slightly up-slope, converging with a vehicular track from your right. This leads through more woodland, past Lady Emma's 1882 Cottage on your right and then through a plantation of pine trees.

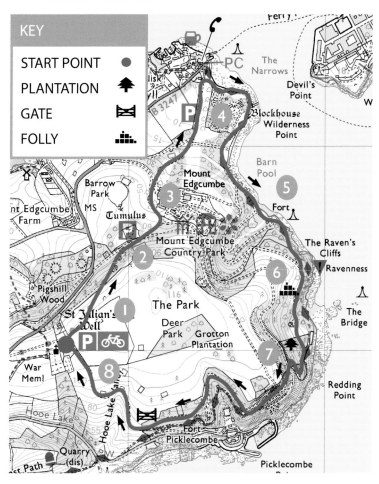

KEY

START POINT	●
PLANTATION	🌲
GATE	⊠
FOLLY	⛫

7) The path doubles back uphill and you must now climb two steep flights of steps, crossing a track midway up and passing through a gate at the top to a roofless grotto with great views out to sea. Past the grotto, a short flight of steps leads down and on through the woodland (ignore a fork to your left), turning inland around a converted fort and tennis courts. Just after the path turns back towards the sea, turn right up a short path leading to a field gate, and left again just before the gate.

8) Continue along the top edge of the wood to a wooden gate and a track leading into the deer park, up quite a long hill, to the church and car park where you started.

PADSTOW

This short and mainly easy walk leads from the town's 15th-century St Petroc's church, past Prideaux Place, a Tudor manor house and its deer park, along a quiet lane to the wide sandy beach at Tregirls Cove.

You'll then follow the coast path beside the picturesque Camel Estuary back to bustling Padstow Harbour. Padstow is one of the few protected anchorages for ships seeking shelter along Cornwall's Atlantic coast, but its usefulness has, since a violent storm in Henry VIII's time, been blighted by the existence of the Doom Bar – a notorious spit of sand lying across the harbour entrance which has caused the beaching, wreck or capsize of around 600 vessels over the past 200 years.

At low tide and in rough weather, the bar can be clearly seen stretching from Tregirls Beach to Trebetherick on the far side of the estuary, and old wrecks are revealed from time to time as the sands shift. In 2010 a few windows were shattered locally when Royal Navy divers tried to blow up the wreck of the barque Antoinette.

A previous attempt to destroy the ship in 1895 is said to have broken every window in Padstow. Every year more than 50,000 tonnes of sand are removed from the estuary by the Harbour Commissioners' two dredgers, Sandsnipe and Mannin.

Legend (and several ballads) relate how the storm which gave rise to the bar was invoked by a mermaid, shot by a fisherman in mistake for a seal.

The walk could easily be extended by continuing from Tregirls Cove seaward past Hawker's Cove and around Stepper Point, but for this gentle stroll we head back alongside the estuary towards Padstow.

The first headland you will pass is Gun Point, where you will see what is left of a Napoleonic gun battery and water tank. These few remains were spared when more recent, Second World War gun emplacements were demolished in 1945. You may still see the old generator shed for WWII searchlights buried in ivy to your right as you descend around the small creek at St George's Well.

A little further on you will reach the Padstow war memorial with its array of commemorative benches, where you can rest and enjoy the fabulous views over the harbour and upper estuary. In summer, classic speedboats, the graceful Jubilee Queen and the Rock Ferry vie for visitor trade and every imaginable water sport is enjoyed along the estuary.

At high water you'll be able to watch the fishing fleet and harbour traffic navigating the channel below you.

THE BASICS

Distance: 3 miles, 4.8km

Gradient: Gentle – one moderate climb at the end with steps

Severity: Easy

Time: 1½ hours

Stiles: Several stiles

Map: OS Explorer 106, Newquay & Padstow

Path description: Quiet lane, sandy field margins, coast path and through town centre

Parking: Padstow Link Road (pay) car park. Follow A389 (from Wadebridge) past turning to the town centre. Turn into large car park (and play area) on your right, just past the fire station. OS 917753 – PL28 8DT

Landscape: Town, farmland and estuary

Nearest refreshment: Numerous pubs and cafés in Padstow

PADSTOW WALK

The Route

1) Take the footpath from the end of the car park furthest from the fire station. Follow the path downhill to a lychgate and into St Petroc's churchyard. The church is usually open to visitors if there is no service taking place and is well worth a visit.

2) On exiting the church, turn right uphill through the churchyard to an iron kissing gate and then turn left up Church Street. Take the first turning on the right onto Tregirls Lane and follow this quiet no-through road leading past Prideaux Manor House on your left (and its deer park opposite), through a stone arch and between high Cornish hedges through farmland for two-thirds of a mile. At the end of the lane turn right into the field just before Tregirls Cottages and then keep left, downhill, with the buildings and field boundary to your left.

3) Just as the track starts to level out, take the narrow path to your right, following the coast path waymark. There is the option to continue ahead here on the farm track for another 50 yards and then cross the sand dunes on your right onto Tregirls Beach. At low tide it is possible to walk most of the way to Padstow on the beach but be warned, this can be quite tiring on the soft sand and rejoining the higher-level coast path may involve a bit of a scramble up a steep sandy path.

4) For those of you on the coast path, you will follow the edge of several arable fields (often planted with cauliflowers) to Gun Point, where the path widens and leads you around a small creek at St George's Well and up to the war memorial and the best view of the day. Beyond the war memorial, the path

forks and you should keep left on the 'main drag' leading to the town and harbour.

5) Just before you reach the harbour you will pass a café and crazy golf course just above the path. Its terrace offers a perfect spot to relax and watch all that is going on in the harbour below you.

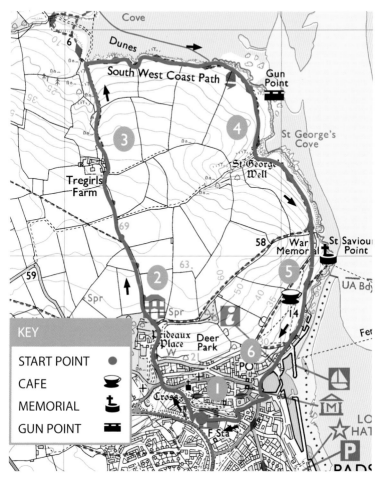

KEY

START POINT •

CAFE ♨

MEMORIAL ⬤

GUN POINT ▬

6) Follow the harbour along two of its sides to the red and white vehicle 'no entry' signs where you take the pedestrian path to your right signed 'Drang'. At the end of the Drang, turn right and then immediately left up Mill Road. Just before the road turns downhill to the right, you will see a wide flight of steps ahead which you should climb. At the top of the path, turn right and continue to the far end of a wooden fence on your left, at which point (hopefully!) you will see a familiar path to your left leading back uphill to the car park.

POLLY JOKE, WEST PENTIRE

THIS SHORT WALK AROUND PENTIRE WEST HEADLAND IS A TONIC AT ANY SEASON BUT ESPECIALLY SO IN MID TO LATE JUNE, WHEN IT OFFERS THE CHANCE TO EXPERIENCE A SPECTACULAR FLOWERING OF POPPIES AND CORN MARIGOLDS.

Once the unintended result of unsprayed winter feed crops, the now famous display is 'managed' successfully by the National Trust and provides not only a sea of red and yellow each summer but also a perfect habitat for skylarks, winter flocks of finches and the rarer corn bunting.

Polly Joke beach is the postcard photographer's dream of a hidden Cornish cove with golden sands, rock pools and little caves occasionally enhanced in winter by cattle straying from the adjacent common.

As with most of the North Cornwall coast, sunsets over the sea can be spectacular, so late afternoon or early evening is an ideal time to visit.

The cliffs you'll pass after leaving Polly Joke Cove are home to a small colony of fulmars, whose aerial prowess is unmatched in the seabird world and can be highly entertaining.

The walk takes you inland past the first of the poppy fields to Treago Mill and the start of Cubert Common, a large expanse of grassy sand dunes and a Bronze Age settlement (there is still a well-defined barrow close to Cubert village).

On reaching Polly Joke beach, you can extend the walk by a mile by continuing west along the coast path for half a mile (keeping the beach to your right) as far as Kelsey Head, where you might be lucky enough to see a grey seal or two fishing between the headland and the little island known as The Chick. (The next island to the east – off Pentire Point East – is known as The Goose.)

On reaching the headland, you will need to retrace your steps to the head of the beach.

THE BASICS

Distance: 2 miles (3 miles including Kelsey Head) 3.2 or 4.8km

Gradient: One steep descent and a few short climbs

Severity: Easy

Time: 1 – 1½ hours

Stiles: None

Map: OS Explorer 104, Redruth & St Agnes

Path description: Farm access tracks, sandy paths and grassy headland

Parking: Public (pay) car park below Bowgie Inn. OS 776607 – TR8 5SE

Landscape: Grassy dune common, small fields, coastal slope and cliff top

Nearest refreshment: Bowgie Inn at start/end of walk. Terrace overlooks sea

POLLY JOKE, WEST PENTIRE WALK

The Route

1) Walk out of the Bowgie Inn Car Park to the road and immediately turn right up the hill signposted Polly Joke and Treago Valley. Passing the 17th-century Manor House and Manor Cottage to your right, keep left up the hill past John Sleep's vintage gramophone and phonograph repair workshop to the Polly Joke Beach Car Park.

2) Keeping Polly Joke long-stay car park on your left, the road becomes a well-defined farm track. This track continues for about three-quarters of a mile with hedges on either side. After a fairly steep descent you will arrive at Treago Mill (a white painted cottage with large fuel tanks in the drive). Just before the entrance to the mill, turn right down a narrow footpath with ivy-clad fences both sides. We often pause here to listen to the birdsong beside the stream.  Continue over a wooden bridge and camping field on the right.

3) The path soon ends at a vehicular access track where you turn right, past the camping field entrance, and bear right into the National Trust car park. You have to ford the stream at this point but it is narrow enough to step across for all but the very smallest legs!

4) Exit the car park through a small pedestrian wooden gate next to a National Trust information board and continue down this sandy path in the direction of the beach, ignoring a branch off to the left. Below, to the right, the stream meanders through banks of trees and expanses of reedy marshland. Just before you reach the beach, you will pass through another wooden gate. Cattle and sheep grazing on the slopes are free to use the beach and often do so in the winter.

5) After enjoying a sandy picnic or a paddle, cross the wooden bridge at the top end of the beach, signposted to West Pentire. Bear left through the kissing gate and after 40 yards bear left again through a gap in the hedge to follow the eastern edge of the creek towards the sea (you have the option to continue straight ahead up the hill here for a short cut back to the pub!). The path leads you through another in-and-out gate and past a tamarisk hedge opening up to spectacular views of the open sea. On reaching a bench the path turns 90 degrees to the right up a short but fairly steep incline.

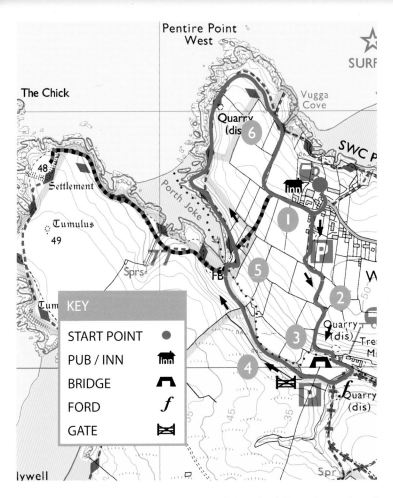

The Chick

Pentire Point West

Vugga Cove

Quarry (dis

SWC P

48

Settlement

Porth Joke

Tumulus
49

Sprs

Tu

FB

KEY

START POINT ●

PUB / INN 🏠

BRIDGE ⌒

FORD *f*

GATE ⬚

Quarry (dis)

Tre
M

Quarry (dis)

lywell

Spr

6) Continue along the coast path, ignoring a fork to the right, past several small quarries. Ahead, the Gannel Estuary soon opens up with impressive views to Pentire Headland, The Goose, and Trevose Lighthouse in the far distance. At the 'cropped' crossroads turn right, keeping the sea on your left. After 200 yards a stone wall should appear on your right. Continue through the blackthorn scrub until you reach a T-junction, where you turn right. The very pink Bowgie Inn is now visible ahead. Just after the next kissing gate, leave the coast path to your left (this is an alternative, longer route back to the pub) and bear right up a long, straight hill. As you approach the top of the hill, you will be surrounded by arable fields which, during early summer, offer an amazing display of poppies and corn marigolds. At the top of hill, turn left towards West Pentire and follow the well-defined track back to the road and the Bowgie Inn.

PORTREATH

ONCE THE 19TH CENTURY'S COPPER CAPITAL OF THE
WORLD, PORTREATH'S QUAINT HARBOUR AND OVERGROWN
TRAMWAYS ARE NOW THE ONLY REMINDERS OF A GREAT
INDUSTRIAL PAST

Two major tramways led from the harbour to Carn Brea in Redruth (part of the Hayle railway) and south to the mining area around Gwennap. This second tramway (the final third of our walk) forms part of the popular Coast to Coast Trail which connects Portreath to Devoran on the south coast (watch out for bikes in summer!).

The walk starts by passing under the Hayle tramway incline and takes you up a beautiful wooded valley to the village of Illogan (pronounced illuggan). It is well worth stopping to explore the peaceful and unusual Illogan churchyard, which is maintained in a wild state by Cornwall Wildlife Trust.

The 16th-century church was relocated in 1846 but permission was refused by Trinity House to demolish the old bell tower, which was considered an important landmark by local seamen, so the church and tower stand 100 yards apart.

Between the two is the remains of an early Celtic cross, and amongst the graves are victims of the plague of 1591, the Cornish composer, Thomas Merritt and an area set aside for 52 war graves (RAF Portreath was Cornwall's largest wartime fighter station).

The walk continues downhill across daffodil fields to join the tramway at Bridge and finishes by taking you along the historic harbour to the car park and large sandy beach (no dogs allowed from Easter to 1 October).

THE BASICS

Distance: 3 miles, 4.8km

Gradient: Mainly gently sloping

Severity: Mainly easy but one short steep and sometimes muddy slope

Time: 1¾ hours

Stiles: Three, but very low (more like granite cattle grids)

Map: OS Explorer 104, Redruth & St Agnes

Path description: Woodland trail, some roads, ex-tramway

Parking: Portreath beach (pay) car park. OS 654453 – TR16 4NN. There is free parking on the adjacent road if you can find a space

Landscape: Wooded valleys and farmland

Nearest refreshment: Atlantic Café Bar (takeaway or eat in) at beach car park. Several other pubs and cafés in the village

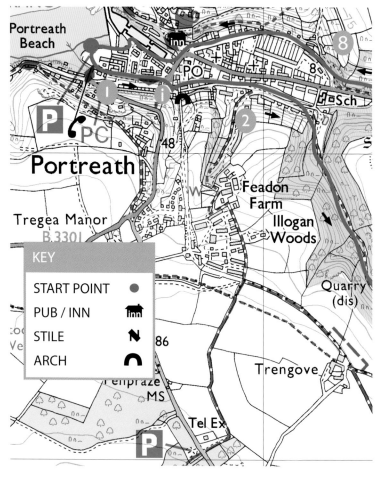

The Route

1) Turn left out of the beach car park along the main road towards Redruth. After 200 yards you will see a blue bus shelter on your right and a large anchor on a plinth. There is an information board here and a road to your right leading across a small stream and through the stone arch which once carried the horse-drawn tramway to Carn Brea.

2) Pass under the arch and continue along Glenfeadon Terrace for 300 yards, past a fork in the road (keep right, past the 'no through road' sign) until the road narrows to become a footpath leading into Illogan Woods. The path leads you through a substantial block wall and over a small stream and then climbs steadily up the wooded valley for about two-thirds of a mile. The woodland is a mixture of ivy-clad oak, beech and holly, with carpets of bluebells in April. We saw several

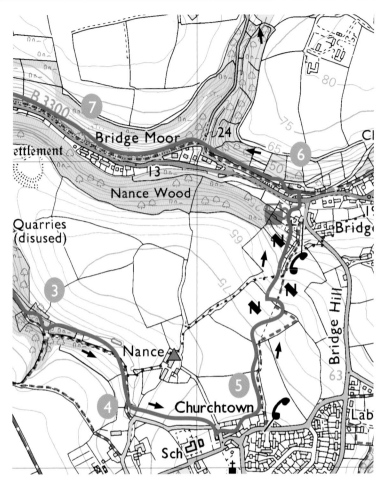

nuthatches here and we were told you should look out for pipistrelle bats on summer evenings.

3) As you near the top of the hill, ignore a turning to the right and bear left past the two sets of granite gateposts. The woodland gradually gives way to farmland to left and right and you'll pass a small man-made lake and a farm on your left before the path ends at a tennis court and gate leading onto a narrow country lane.

4) Turn left up the lane towards Illogan village, past the village hall, to a T-junction where you turn left past a row of stone cottages on your left and a stone wall and trees to your right. Orientate yourself here because we are about to take you off-route to explore the churchyard, whose entrance you will see to your right at the T-junction.

PORTREATH WALK

Having done your exploring, recommence the walk past the cottages just mentioned to a second T-junction where you turn left at a property called Roseland. After a hundred yards, turn left opposite Tangye Close down a grassy footpath between two houses.

5) The path leads downhill through three daffodil fields in the direction of RAF Portreath, whose hangars you will see on the hillside opposite. The hedge will initially be on your right, then left and then right again – separated in each case by a low, granite stile. In the third field you will follow the hedge along two of its sides until reaching a final stile on your right next to an electricity pole.

6) Cross this stile and follow the line of electricity poles downhill (it can be slippery here) to a gate leading onto a tarmac drive. Continue down the drive and turn

left at the bottom, past the Bridge Inn to a T-junction. Turn left along the main road to Portreath (taking great care as there is no pavement) and after 30 yards cross the road and turn right up a lane signed 'Portreath Tramroad'. After another 50 yards, double back to your left, signed to Portreath.

7) The old tramroad will lead you the mile and a quarter back to Portreath, initially through woodland then (as the path merges with a small public road) along a long line of untidy but interesting back gardens including (probably) Cornwall's smallest massage clinic!

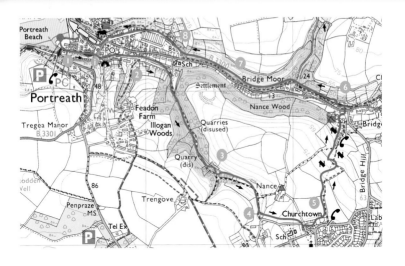

8) You finally rejoin the main road at the Portreath Arms. Turn right towards the bus shelter and anchor sculpture from which you set out – but before you get there, turn right into Forth-An-Nance Road (towards the harbour). Follow the footpath along the left side of the harbour until it ends, then pass to the left of the Waterside Inn and immediately right to a set of steps which will lead you back into the beach car park.

RAME HEAD

RAME HEAD, FAMILIAR TO GENERATIONS OF RETURNING
SAILORS, IS A DISTINCTIVE, DOME-SHAPED HEADLAND ON
THE WESTERN APPROACH TO PLYMOUTH SOUND.

The autumnal combination of cold morning air on a warm sea often creates the illusion that it is an island when first visible to approaching ships. On 20 April 1770, a similarly shaped headland in south-eastern Australia was the very first place to be given a name (Rame Head) by Captain Cook on sighting the new continent. His ship, Endeavour, had sailed from Plymouth two years earlier and the Rame headland would have been the ship's company's last distinct view of the British mainland.

Our short walk takes you around the headland, with dramatic coastal scenery, through daffodil fields and past the 13th-century Rame Church over initially easy terrain but with a longish climb at the end from Polhawn Battery where it is steep in a few places. There is an optional scramble up to the medieval chapel on completion of the round walk; quite a tough climb, but well worth the effort if you have the energy left for it.

The chapel, dedicated to St Michael, is thought to date from the late 14th century and may have replaced a hermitage (the headland and manor were given to Tavistock Abbey by Earl Ordulf in 981).

During the Iron Age, a rampart and ditch (still clearly visible) were constructed, probably

to create a place of safety or status rather than as a settlement. In the 15th and 16th centuries a watch was maintained on Rame Head and beacons were lit to warn of approaching ships. More recently it was the site of an anti-submarine gun in World War I and a concrete gun emplacement and mobile radar station in World War II.

In 2004, the Leander-class frigate HMS Scylla was sunk to create an artificial diving reef to the west of Rame Head. Launched in 1970, her colourful career had included colliding with the Tamar Ferry and a Royal Fleet Auxilliary vessel and colliding with an Icelandic gunboat during the Cod War.

THE BASICS

Distance: 2.5 miles, 4km

Gradient: Mostly easy or moderate but steep in a few places

Severity: Moderate

Time: 1½ hours

Stiles: None but some steps

Map: OS Explorer 108, Lower Tamar Valley & Plymouth

Path description: Coast path, farmland and minor roads

Parking: Rame Head (free) car park next to National Coastwatch Station

OS 420488 – PL10 1LH

Landscape: Farmland; coast

Nearest food: Various pubs and cafés in Cawsand

RAME HEAD WALK

The Route

1) Exit the car park through a kissing gate with the Coastwatch Station on your left. (The National Coastwatch Institution is a voluntary organisation which mans the old coastguard lookout daily from 8am to 8pm – or dusk – monitoring activity on the water and coastpath, alerting rescue services and providing information and assistance to walkers. There are public toilets at the rear of the building.)

2) Head down the grassy slope towards the ruined chapel for about 150 yards and, just before you reach the defensive ditch and two viewpoint benches on your left, turn left to join the coast path towards Penlee Point and the entrance to Plymouth Sound. The coastal slope is grazed in winter by Dartmoor ponies.

3) The path climbs gently through an area of gorse and blackthorn with glorious views to the Yealm Estuary and Bolt Head. On a clear day you should easily make out the Eddystone lighthouse nine miles to the south. Continue past a crossroads in the path and after another half-mile turn left through a kissing gate signposted to Rame Church.

4) Follow the path uphill, keeping the hedge on your left to a gate ahead into a narrow lane. Turn left along the lane to a T-junction (just past the church), where you turn right to continue the walk or left if you wish to cut it short and return the half-mile along the road to the car park (easier but dull!). The church is open to visitors and is well worth a visit. The tower, north aisle and chancel are thought to date from 1259, with the south transept added in the 15th century.

5) After several bends in the road, you will pass two brick pillars on your left leading to Rame Barton. Just past this entrance, turn left up a tarmac lane past an old stable yard to your right and some modern farm buildings on your left. Follow the lane for half a mile, enjoying a sweeping view of the coast west across Whitsand Bay to Looe Island, Mevagissey and (in clear weather) the Lizard Peninsula. If the wind is from the south-west, you may also see paragliders, for whom the long stretch of coastal slope provides good soaring conditions.

6) Just before you reach the 'main' road, turn sharp left down the metalled drive to Polhawn Fort, a Napoleonic gun battery that was never used (except briefly as a military prison), probably never armed and which now serves as an upmarket wedding venue. Bear right at the first fork in the lane down an access road to

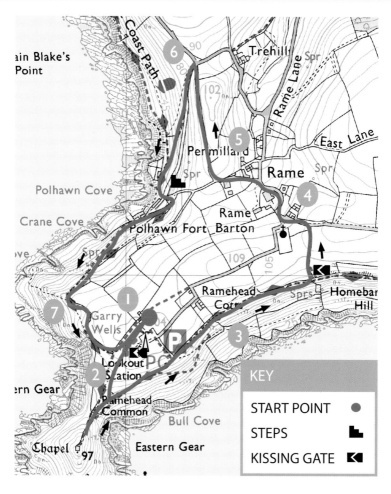

Polhawn Cottages and, just before reaching the first cottage, bear left along the narrow coast path, passing along the back of the houses. At the top of a flight of steps you cross the fort access road and are faced with another longer set of steps leading to a T-junction where you turn right through a small gate.

7) After a further half-mile (often uphill) you will be greeted by the welcome sight of the Rame Head chapel ahead.

When you reach the finger post below the Coastwatch Station, you have the option of visiting the chapel on the point. The climb to the top is uneven and slippery but the reward is considerable. Photos simply can't do justice to the experience of looking down from the little ruin on a fine day.

ROCK

This is a walk in John Betjeman's favourite part of Cornwall and, if the sun is shining, you will soon discover why. There is something about the Camel Estuary that never fails to lifts one's spirits.

Being predominantly sandy, it is a walk we rely on when the rest of Cornwall is waterlogged and muddy.

The start is close to the landing point of the ferry from Padstow so arrival by boat is an option.

The route leads along the sea front and then around and across St Enodoc Golf Course. The course was designed by James Braid in 1907 and has been voted Cornwall's best golf course on the 'Top 100 Golf Courses' website.

Beyond the golf course, you will come to St Enodoc church. St Enodoc (or Guenedoc) was a Welsh hermit who is said to have baptised converts in the sixth century at the nearby Jesus Holy Well.

Originating in the 12th century, and largely reconstructed some 300 years later, this delightful small 'chapel of ease' was almost completely buried by sand during a violent storm in the 1500s. The story goes that services continued to be conducted once a year (access was gained through a hole in the roof) so that the church could legally continue to collect a tithe from surrounding farms. In 1863 the sand was removed and the church restored to its present condition.

Many of John Betjeman's poems were inspired by the church and its surrounding coastline, which he had known and loved from childhood. Trebetherick became his second home and his grave and a modest headstone can be found in the churchyard.

The walk then takes you onto the beach at Daymer Bay, popular with bathers and kite surfers (a small shop, café and toilets can be found at the back of the beach car park). The coast path leads around the base of Brea Hill – somewhat hilly and precipitous initially – but with an option here, except near high tide, to follow the beach some or all of the way back to Rock. Be warned, however, that the sand can be quite soft in places, which can make walking hard work.

It is worth checking tide times and scheduling your walk to coincide with half-tide or lower if you are nervous about the vertiginous stretch of path and wish to avoid it!

Be aware, too, that although bathing at Daymer Bay is reasonably safe when the tide is in, strong currents along the estuary make swimming dangerous elsewhere and at low tide.

THE BASICS

Distance: 3 miles, 4.8km

Gradient: Gently sloping but with two moderate hills

Severity: Mostly easy

Time: 1½ hours

Stiles: None

Map: OS Explorer 106, Newquay & Padstow

Path description: Grassy and sandy paths, minor roads and beach

Parking: Follow signs to Rock and continue to end of road. OS 928758 – PL27 6FD

Landscape: Golf links, sandy estuary

Nearest food: The Rock Inn or Blue Tomato Café

ROCK WALK

The Route

1) Leave the car park by the entrance road and continue alongside the road for quarter of a mile to a turning left to St Enodoc Golf Club (80 yards beyond where the pavement ends). Follow this road uphill and, just before the barrier at the golf club entrance, turn left onto a residential lane and after 20 yards turn right down a narrow path through high undergrowth.

   Follow the path (ignoring a fork off to the left) uphill until you emerge onto the golf course with views ahead of you to Stepper Point and the entrance to the Camel Estuary.

2) The path is now clearly marked with white stones, which lead initially along the left-hand edge of the golf course and then to your right across the course in the general direction of Brea Hill. (Brea Hill is an isolated, dome-shaped hill at the further end  of the golf course. Your route will eventually lead you to the right-hand side of the hill and then in an anti-clockwise direction around it.) There are a number of warnings to look out in all directions for low and/or stray golf balls!

3) The path emerges onto a tarmac service road and parking area where you turn left. You are immediately faced with a choice (clearly marked on the road) of a left turn towards the beach (avoiding the hill and vertiginous section – but missing the beautiful church) or a right turn to the church. If you take the short route (left), follow the stone markers across the golf course and then continue towards the sea until you reach an obvious valley running from right to left through the dunes. Turn left here to join the main (coast path) route back to the start.

4) If you have turned right to the church, cross the stone bridge and immediately turn left, following the white markers on the left of the fairway. The route passes to the left of the church – but do take the short diversion to look around as it is a highlight of the walk. Beyond the church, continue along the gravel path until it splits and you should take the left fork between high blackthorn scrub. Continue to follow the white markers, which lead eventually to the coast path, onto which you turn left just above Daymer Beach.

5) The coast path leads you across a small bridge and then up a sandy slope onto the path leading around Brae Hill (you can take the beach route from here below half tide).

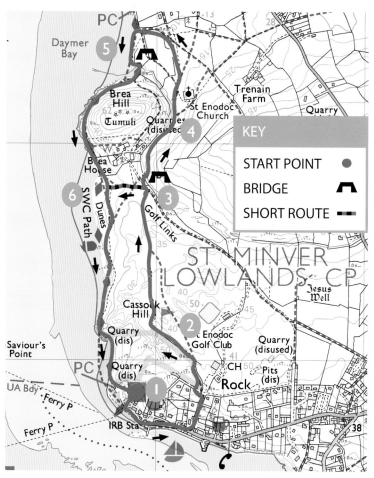

KEY

START POINT ●

BRIDGE ⌐⌐

SHORT ROUTE ▬ ▬

6) There are a number of routes back through the dunes which it would be nearly impossible to describe, but we chose the route which runs along the only obvious long valley. There is a short climb (up to the left) at the end of the valley before the path turns right downhill towards Padstow (across the estuary). Ignore a flight of wooden steps down to the beach as the path leads into the car park just beyond them.

ST ANTHONY'S HEAD

IN CONTRAST TO ITS FAMOUS NEIGHBOUR AT LIZARD POINT, ST ANTHONY'S HEADLAND LIES WELL OFF THE TRAIL OF ALL BUT THE MOST DETERMINED TOURIST.

The remote promontory at the southern tip of the beautiful Roseland Peninsula provides a varied and enjoyable walk, contrasting the gentle slopes and sheltered waters of the Carrick Roads on its northern side with the craggy cliffs and open sea to its south.

The headland is important historically as it commands one side of the entrance to Falmouth Harbour and was the site of a number of fortifications dating from the 19th century to the Second World War. Its armaments were removed in the 1950s but much of the battery, including gun emplacements, magazine and observation post remain. Former officers' quarters and an artillery workshop have been converted into holiday cottages by the National Trust.

St Anthony's Head lighthouse can only be glimpsed from the path (it is also let for holidays) and will be familiar to many as the Fraggle Rock Lighthouse from the Jim Henson television series.

It was built in 1835, when it was lit by eight oil lamps, and was manned until 1987. The light has a red sector to warn navigators of the dangerous Manacles Rocks, on which many ships have foundered and many hundreds of sailors have perished.

The first part of the walk leads towards the sheltered anchorage of the Percuil River with views to St Mawes Castle and the picture-perfect waterfront of this once poor fishing

village, whose humble cottages now command inflated prices as second homes. The coast path ends at the very grand Place House, home to generations of the Spry family, and the 12th-century Place Church which is open to visitors.

From Place House you are faced with a long but not very steep climb along a little-used lane and then across a small field to the coast path on the southern side of the peninsula. There is one more moderate climb and a couple of stiles before the path levels out along the pretty cliff top, leading you back to the headland and battery buildings.

THE BASICS

Distance: 3¼ miles, 5.2km

Gradient: Gently sloping but with two moderate climbs

Severity: Moderate

Time: 1¾ hours

Stiles: 2

Map: OS Explorer 105, Falmouth & Mevagissey

Path description: Coast path – uneven in places, farm access track & very minor road

Parking: Follow signs, initially to St Mawes and then to St Anthony's Head and continue to the end of the road. OS 848313 – TR2 5HA

Landscape: Channel coast, estuary, scrub, wood and farmland

Nearest food: The Garden Tea Room, St Anthony's Head (Sun to Fri); The Royal Standard, Gerrans

ST ANTHONY'S HEAD WALK

The Route

1) Leave the car park at its far end where a path leads downhill to the right through woodland signed 'to the lighthouse'. Keep right at the first fork (unless you wish to explore the battery and bird hide) and, just before the path ends at the lighthouse gates, double back to your right onto the coast path.

2) The Carrick Roads now stretch off to your left with Pendennis Castle and Falmouth Harbour over your left shoulder and St Mawes with its pretty 16th-century castle ahead of you across the Percuil Estuary.

3) Follow the path past the old paraffin store, through a white gate and around the two beautiful golden sandy beaches at Great Molunan to an ancient stand of pine trees on Carricknath Point.

4) The path leads along the bottom of a large sloping field and about 75 yards before its end you should follow the mown track uphill to the top right-hand corner. Pass through the wicket gate at the top and follow the yellow waymark arrow which directs you ahead down the left-hand edge of another field and onto a farm access track at the bottom. Turn right onto the track and follow it through an area of mature woodland with glimpses of the Percuil River to your left.

5) After about 300 yards take the right-hand fork signed to Church and Place Quay and, after another 150 yards, go left onto a narrower path (with a yellow waymark arrow) leading past some beehives and down steps to the church.

The church contains memorials to many members of the Spry family and is well worth exploring. After leaving the church, continue through the graveyard, passing a medieval (empty!) stone coffin and, on reaching the narrow public lane, turn right uphill and follow the road for about a third of a mile.

Turning left onto the lane would lead you after a short distance to the ferry landing stage. This could be an alternative starting point for the walk if you chose to arrive by (summer) ferry from St Mawes.

6) Just beyond the brow of the hill, very shortly after passing the entrance gates to Kitpurva on your left, you will see a gap in the hedge and a stile to your right with

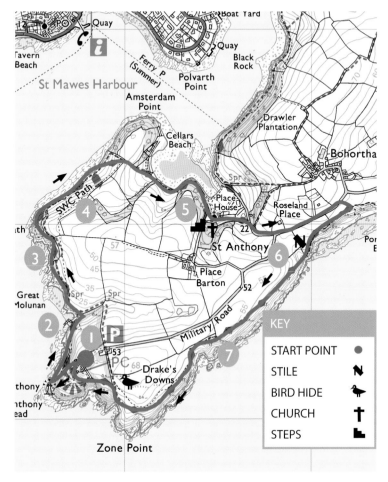

a finger post directing you downhill towards the sea across an arable field. At the bottom of the field you should turn right onto the coast path (if you are feeling very energetic, you might wish to continue straight ahead down the steep path and steps to the beautiful and little frequented Porthbeor Beach).

7) The coast path now leads you back the mile and a bit to St Anthony's Head battery, where you can relax (if it's not too windy) and enjoy views to the Lizard, Swanpool Beach, Pendennis Castle, Falmouth Docks and across the Carrick Roads to St Mawes (a 'toposcope' on the summit is engraved with arrows pointing to the various landmark features). Beyond the battery, you will pass toilets and the old officers' quarters before reaching the car park from which you set out.

TEHIDY

THE POWERFUL BASSET FAMILY OWNED THE GREAT MANOR OF
TEHIDY FROM NORMAN TIMES (SIR FRANCIS BASSET OPENED
CORNWALL'S FIRST HORSE-DRAWN TRAMWAY TO TRANSPORT
COPPER ORE FROM POLDICE TO PORTREATH IN 1808)

In 1916, when the family's fortunes (and popularity) took a dive and the house was sold. It briefly became a TB hospital but suffered a serious fire a few weeks after opening.

The great house, built in the 1860s, had 40 bedrooms and a drawing room renowned for its gold ceiling. The surrounding estate was planted to provide hunting for the baron as well as 400 acres for food production. It is now maintained by Cornwall Council as a popular country park.

The Tehidy estate includes one of Cornwall's largest woodlands (the North Cliff Plantation is famous for its spring show of bluebells) as well as several beautiful lakes and some extremely tame wildlife (take along some bird nuts for the squirrels!).

To protect the wildfowl, dogs are excluded from the lake areas, but an alternative route is available.

The full walk takes in a mile and a half of coastal path from the spectacular Basset's Cove along some of the highest cliffs on the North Cornish coast, with views to Godrevy in the west and the Basset Memorial on Carn Brea to the south. The coast path is quite level but very exposed to the wind and comes close to the cliff edge in a few places, so keep your dog and/or children under suitable control.

Although the walking is all easy, there are well-signed shorter walks within the park,

beginning with an almost flat, wheelchair-accessible walk around the lakes and increasing in length (and very slightly in difficulty) to around two miles.

THE BASICS

Distance: 4 miles, 6.4km

Gradient: Mostly flat or gentle

Severity: Easy

Time: 2 hours

Stiles: None

Map: OS Explorer 104, Redruth & St Agnes

Path description: Well-made woodland trails with some coast path (easy) and half a mile on grass field-edge

Parking: Tehidy Country Park South Drive (free) car park. OS 650433 – TR14 0EZ

Landscape: Woodland, coast path, farmland

Dogs: Prohibited around lakes

Nearest food: Tehidy Café at start/end of walk. Open 7 days 1000 to 1600

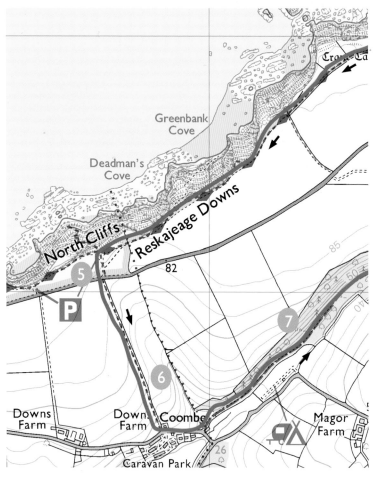

1) Enter the country park through two large stone pillars and immediately turn right past the visitor centre and café. Keep right here, following the sign to North Cliff Plantation.

2) The path soon merges with an estate road, which you follow uphill for 100 yards. Go through the wicket gate ahead of you, signposted 'Footpath to Tehidy Country Park', and continue for a further 150 yards to a crossroads where you turn left for North Cliffs. You will have a good view here of what remains of the Great House – surrounded by some slightly less impressive 20th-century architecture. Keep left along the wooden fence and look out on your right for the 200-year-old twisted beech tree. Children will have fun looking for the earliest date carved into its bark.

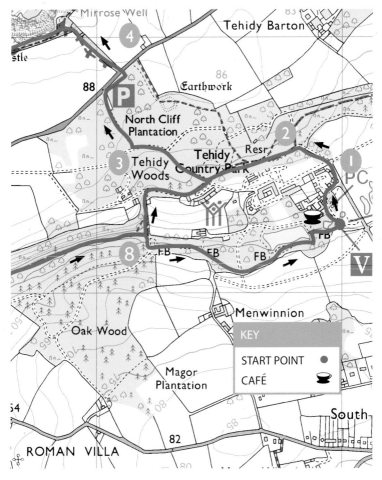

3) Some 200 yards beyond the twisted beech, the estate road converges from the left at an old gate and there is a turning to the right marked with a red arrow. Follow this path into the North Cliff Plantation – an old beech and oak woodland with carpets of bluebells in spring. You'll pass a spectacular twisted root on your left and after quarter of a mile you should take the right-hand fork marked with a red arrow and blue 'P'. Follow this path to North Cliff car park.

Continue through the car park, turning right alongside the coast road for 50 yards, and then take the public byway on your left which leads you to the cliff-top car park at Basset's Cove.

4) Turn left and follow the coast path west for 1¼ miles. The third gate you come to

leads into a small car park. Turn left here, crossing the road onto a waymarked public path which leads downhill away from the coast and alongside grazing land.

5) Ahead of you is the western edge of Camborne, with Redruth to your left and Carn Brea hill and the Basset Memorial in between.

6) The path continues downhill in a straight line for about a third of a mile to a wooden gate leading onto a country lane and mobile home park opposite. Turn left onto the road and at the first bend take the footpath to your left, marked West Drive to Tehidy. There's a tea room here which opens at weekends in the winter and every day in summer from 10 to 5.30pm.

7) Now follow the woodland trail for about a mile, ignoring a turn to Oak Wood on your right and another trail which diverges to your left, until you reach the end of the path at a T-junction. If you have a dog in your party you should turn left at this point up the hill and follow the trail, keeping right at all times until you find yourself back at the twisted beech tree and can retrace your earlier steps back to the visitor centre.

8) Those of you without a dog should turn right at the T-junction past the carved otters, across the Otter Bridge, which is constructed of massive granite boulders, and immediately left, signposted to South Drive and lakes. From here all trails will lead you back to the car park but on our walk we chose to keep right, close to the edge of the woodland and then along the right-hand edge of the big lake.

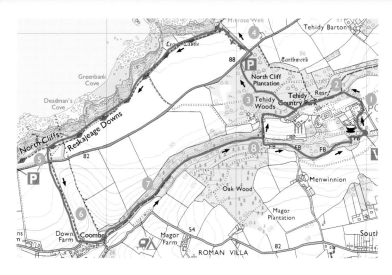

The lakes were for us the highlight of this walk, almost tripping over tame swans and squirrels on the path. We're not sure what council policy is on feeding the wildlife but the children we watched feeding nuts to the squirrels were clearly having a great time.

TRELISSICK

TRELISSICK HOUSE AND ITS SURROUNDING 376 ACRES OF GARDENS AND WOODLAND WERE GIVEN TO THE NATIONAL TRUST BY THE COPELAND FAMILY IN 1955.

The house enjoys commanding views to the south across the Carrick Roads and is surrounded on three sides by the River Fal and the Channals and Lamouth Creeks. The formal gardens are open all year for an admission fee and contain an impressive collection of 'tender and exotic' plants as well as a large variety of rhododendrons, azaleas and hydrangeas.

The former carriage drive, built by the estate's owners along the riverside, now provides a popular and reasonably easy walk through the mature woodlands which cloak the banks of the Fal River along most of its upper reaches.

The walk starts from the National Trust car park near the house and descends across parkland to a creek-side beach and the start of the riverside walk. Look out for a variety of wading birds both here and along the shore of Lamouth Creek towards the end of the walk.

Below you, through the trees, you will pass the rafts and lines of grey buoys which make up the Fal Mussel Farm and, a little further on, the landing pontoons for passenger ferries linking Falmouth, Truro and St Mawes to the National Trust gardens.

The trail crosses a road just above the King Harry car ferry, which provides the only road link to the Roseland Peninsula south of Truro. As it runs on chains, the ferry's owners have sought to re-designate the service as a 'ferry bridge' rather than as a vessel (which might be liable to pay passenger dues to the harbour authority!).

Beyond the King Harry Ferry Bridge, the path sides become less steep and you may see one or more very large ships moored on the river to your right. Since the start of the global recession, a great many ships have been laid up around the world waiting for work, and up to ten at any time have been moored along this stretch of river, providing a welcome cash boost to the harbour authority but rather spoiling the view from the Viscount Falmouth's country seat at Tregothnan on the hill to their left.

To the right of the moored ships you should be able to see the landing pontoons of the Smugglers Cottage pub at Tolverne. General Eisenhower stayed in this picture postcard thatched inn whilst he saw off 27,000 American troops during the D-Day invasion from the beach below the pub.

THE BASICS

Distance: 2½ miles, 4km

Gradient: Mostly gently sloping. One quite long climb at the end

Severity: Easy

Time: 1½ hours

Stiles: None

Map: OS Explorer 105, Falmouth & Mevagissey

Path description: Parkland and a well-maintained woodland trail

Parking: Trelissick Gardens (pay) car park (free in evening and to NT members) OS 836397 – TR3 6QL

Landscape: Parkland and steeply sloping river and creek-side woodland

Nearest food: National Trust Crofter's Café & Barn Restaurant. Punchbowl and Ladle at Penelewey (TR3 6QY)

TRELISSICK WALK

The Route

1) From the green car park kiosk, take the short road signposted 'Woodland Walk' which leads to a gate and cattle grid. Beyond the gate you will see the Fal Estuary – better known as the Carrick Roads – leading away to the sea between the headlands of St Anthony and Pendennis. Take the right-hand of the two grassy paths leading towards the estuary and follow it downhill through the grazed parkland to a small length of beach at the very bottom.

2) Turn left onto the path that runs above the beach and, just after the seat sculpted in the shape of a fish, you will pass through a wooden gate leading onto the woodland trail.

3) The old carriage drive takes you around the headland and along the riverside for ¾ mile with interesting views or glimpses (depending on the season) through the large, ancient and beautiful beech, oak and (younger) sycamore trees.

4) Just after the zigzag path on your right to the ferry landing stage, the path descends to the road above the King Harry Ferry terminus. (There is the option – if it is open – to enter the garden here (currently £8 adults and £4 children) and take a shorter and/or more meandering route back through the formal gardens.)

5) To continue the walk, cross over the road and climb the quite steep flights of steps opposite. There is a bench at the top where you can catch your breath and eat your mid-walk refreshments! The path continues through more woodland, with a good showing of spring bluebells, following the bank of the Fal past the big ship moorings and Tolverne jetties and then along the peaceful backwater of Lamouth Creek.

6) At the head of the creek take the left-hand path signposted to Trelissick. There is the option to extend the walk by about a mile by continuing across the little bridge and along the opposite shore of the creek to Roundwood Quay (another

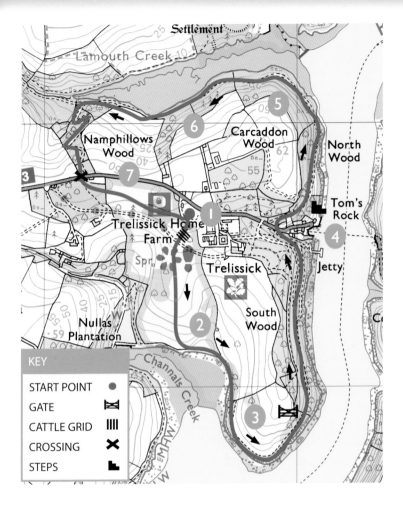

KEY

START POINT	●
GATE	⬁
CATTLE GRID	‖‖‖
CROSSING	✕
STEPS	⌐

of the D-Day embarkation points), returning the same way. The path now leads uphill along a series of switchbacks. It is quite a long hill but not especially steep and you are rewarded near the top with a bench offering a wonderful view of the creek with Roundwood Quay, the Fal and the Tregothnan Estate beyond.

7) At the top of the hill you will come to a gate, where you cross the road to the Old Lodge (this is a fast, narrow road with no footway, so dogs and children should be very carefully supervised). Turn left around the Old Lodge along a stony path leading to a wicket gate into a field. Bear right across the field to a stand of oak trees. The grassy path converges with and then runs parallel to a small estate road.

The path ends at the gate and cattle grid from where you began the walk.

TREVOSE HEAD

THIS IS AN EASY SHORT WALK (WITH JUST ONE LONG BUT GENTLE CLIMB) AND ONE THAT CAN HARDLY BE BEATEN FOR ITS VARIETY OF ROCKY COASTLINE, CLIFFS, WILD FLOWERS AND PICTURE PERFECT SANDY COVES.

Trevose Headland is privately owned and accessible via a toll road (£3.50 at the time of writing). Payment of the toll entitles you to park for the day on the headland as well as in the Booby's Bay summer beach car park (actually located midway across the headland but within fairly easy walking distance (300–400 yards) of Mother Ivey's Bay on the north side and the bigger surfing beaches of Booby's Bay and Constantine Bay to the south). The walk can be started from either car park but the directions we've given begin and end at the headland car park by Trevose Lighthouse.

Beyond the car park, there is the smaller promontory of Dinas Head to explore should you still have the time and energy after completing the two-mile walk.

Soon after the start of the walk you will come to the Round Hole. This is one of a number of blowhole craters to be found along the North Cornish coast, created by the collapse of a sea cave followed by millennia of erosion by wave action. The resulting pit, 100 feet deep with a tunnel connecting it to the sea at high tide, is extraordinarily dramatic but also quite hazardous to unwary children and dogs (as are the adjacent cliffs), so take extreme care.

The walk continues to Booby's Bay, where it turns inland across the neck of the headland to one of the most beautiful small beaches in Cornwall at Mother Ivey's Bay. From here you turn left along the coast path towards the striking new Padstow lifeboat station. This

space-age pod on stilts houses the latest Tamar Class lifeboat and is open to the public on weekdays from 10am to 4pm (this involves a short but worthwhile diversion from your coast path route).

Beyond the lifeboat station you re-enter an area of heathland and will soon notice the white tower of Trevose Lighthouse rising from the gorse ahead. In summer you are likely to see martins skimming low over the heath and to be serenaded by the twitter of skylarks hovering invisibly above you.

The lighthouse was built in 1847 and at that time was the only light between Land's End and Lundy. It was automated in 1995 and the keepers' accommodation is now converted into three holiday apartments.

THE BASICS

Distance: 2 miles, 3.2km

Gradient: Gently sloping

Severity: Easy

Time: 1¼ hours

Stiles: 5

Map: OS Explorer 106, Newquay & Padstow

Path description: Grassy coastal paths and tarmac lane

Parking: Trevose Headland car park (pay by toll). From Padstow, take the B3276 towards Newquay. Trevose Head is signposted (on the right) after 2 miles – OS 852763 – PL28 8SL

Landscape: Heath, farmland, rocky coastline and sandy beaches

Nearest food: The Harlyn Inn, Harlyn Bay

TREVOSE HEAD WALK

The Route

1) From the corner of the car park furthest from the lighthouse, take the gravel path seawards to a stile in the barbed-wire fence. Turn left over the stile onto the coast path (you will be circumnavigating the headland in an anti-clockwise direction).

A short distance beyond the stile, the path splits to either side of the Round Hole. Take the path to the left of the hole to get the best view from the crater's edge, but do take great care! Beyond the Round Hole follow the line of wooden posts downhill to the waymark where the path turns left along the coast.

2) Continue on the coast path until, just before you reach the first of a line of four big houses, you come to a couple of benches and a stone wall. Take the path inland here with the wall (and a golf green) to your right. The path takes you past the Booby's Bay Car Park. At the T-junction, turn right along the toll road.

3) After 200 yards (just before Trevose Farm) you will see an entrance gate on your left with notices saying 'Mother Ivey's Cottage', 'No Entry' and 'Access to Houses Only'. We are assured by the landowner that you may take this path which leads, passing a corrugated steel barn on your left, a short distance to Mother Ivey's Bay.

4) At the end of this access road, you will see ahead of you a path leading down to the beach and, to the left of Little Treharock Cottage, the start of the coast path taking you back to Trevose Head.

5) If you have brought refreshments with you or just want to take the weight off your feet, the coast path above the beach is an ideal spot to rest on one of the benches overlooking Mother Ivey's Bay, with the lifeboat house and Merope Rocks to your left, Gulland Rock out to sea and Pentire Point and The Rumps away to your right. In spring and early summer, the tamarisk hedge behind you will be complemented by an array of wild flowers including sea pink (thrift), yellow kidney vetch, sea campion and white scurvy grass along under the hedge.

Now follow the coast path towards the lifeboat station, passing the striking art

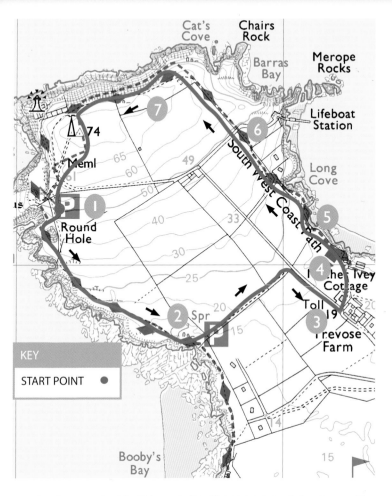

deco house on the cliff which was built by Rick Stein's father before the war. After the second stile you turn left along the lane for a very short distance; you will find the start of the path again on your right after about 10 yards. We were delayed here by a friendly (and hungry) robin and an equally friendly grey pony.

6)   A little further up the hill the path crosses the road to the lifeboat station. This offers another possible diversion and is sufficiently interesting to justify the extra few hundred yards even if the boathouse is closed.

7)   To continue the walk, cross the road and the two stiles and continue on the coast path, which will lead you past the lighthouse and back to your car park.

ABOUT THE AUTHOR

Life changed for John and Vicky in 2001. Whilst John began a (fourth) career as skipper of the Fowey to Mevagissey passenger ferry, Vicky and a work colleague decided (on a bit of a whim and with the minimum of spousal consultation) to embark on an end to end walk of the 258 mile Cornish Coast Path.

We had never been 'serious' walkers (anything more than 5 miles had us creaking at various seams) so we divided the walk into chunks just sufficient to justify a good pub lunch or beach picnic each Sunday. Our only rule was that we walked in all weather. So began a habit that lasted for 13 years and which has fostered an intimate connection with our beautiful county which only walking through (or canoeing around) it can achieve.

There were, of course, the idyllic summer days (a beach picnic in St Ives with an especially good bottle of wine - and the wide, wild sky and almost infinite view from the summit of the Cheesewring), but our most memorable moments were just as often the wettest (attempting to dry out by a barely lit stove in the Smuggler's Inn) or windiest (the cliff path where Grace was blown off her feet) and those which showed off the sea in its more animated lights and moods.

We are not fit (or young) and walking does not have to be strenuous or taken too seriously. We'd just like you to know that there is so much to see and smell and be part of along the paths and by-ways of Cornwall which you will never see or smell or be part of from your car or crowded beach.

JOHN & VICKY WOOD.